YOUR PREACHING
MATTERS

Includes Resources to Help You Plan and
Prepare Transformational Sermons

Register This New Book

Benefits of Registering*

- ✓ FREE **replacements** of lost or damaged books
- ✓ FREE **audiobook** – *Pilgrim's Progress,* audiobook edition
- ✓ FREE information about new titles and other **freebies**

www.anekopress.com/new-book-registration

*See our website for requirements and limitations.

YOUR PREACHING
MATTERS

How to Prepare Sermons
that Cut to the Heart

J. A. JOHNSON
B. K. WOOLSEY

www.genesiscollegeandseminary.com

Your Preaching Matters

© 2025 by J. A. Johnson and B. K. Woolsey

All rights reserved. Published 2025.

Cover Designer: J. Martin

Editor: Paul Miller

Aneko Press

www.anekopress.com

Aneko Press, Life Sentence Publishing, and our logos are trademarks of

Life Sentence Publishing, Inc.
203 E. Birch Street
P.O. Box 652
Abbotsford, WI 54405

RELIGION / Christian Ministry / Preaching

Paperback ISBN: 979-8-88936-521-1

eBook ISBN: 979-8-88936-522-8

10   9   8   7   6   5   4   3   2   1

Available where books are sold

Contents

Foreword

Several years ago, my brother, Dave, was wrestling with whether or not to accept an invitation he had received to join the faculty of the seminary from which he had graduated. If he accepted, he would have to leave his role as a professor of New Testament at a prominent Christian college on the Eastern Seaboard. He asked me to pray for him, and then he said, "I want to make sure that I do not leave for the wrong reasons. I remember Paul Borden's sermon on 2 Samuel 11-12 and how we need to learn to accept what God in His grace has given us and what God in His grace has not."

I was stunned. My brother and I had both been present when Paul Borden preached this sermon on 2 Samuel 11-12 in a local church not far from where we lived at the time, but it had been more than a decade since we had heard it! After our conversation ended, I was struck by the lasting power of a well-crafted sermon. Certainly the Spirit had brought it to my brother's mind, but I am convinced that Dave remembered it so vividly because the sermon was clear, compelling, and faithful to the text. Sermons like this do not happen by chance. They are the result of a preparation process that seeks to interpret Scripture accurately, communicate it compellingly, and apply it insightfully.

The volume you are about to read provides a full-but-concise approach to sermon writing that reflects such a preparation process. I urge you to read it carefully. Quite frankly, I did not expect to write the previous sentence. I'm suspicious of new books on preaching. What can one say that Haddon Robinson and Tim Keller and Bryan Chapell have not already said in their classic volumes on preaching? Robinson's *Biblical Preaching* is now in its fourth edition, and I wrote an endorsement, which appears on the back cover, claiming that the book will serve both veteran and aspiring preachers.

So why bother with this volume by Drs. Johnson and Woolsey? The reason to read it closely is its genius in distilling the insights of some of the best preachers – and teachers of preachers – into a crystal-clear sermon preparation process. Along the way, it will point you to Haddon Robinson's Big Idea approach, Tim Keller's emphasis on gospel-centered preaching, and Eugene Lowry's preaching loop. Yet it does more than rehash the insights of leading preachers. It weaves these insights into a thorough, yet flexible, process for writing a sermon. For example, Johnson and Woolsey encourage three-point sermons since they are more manageable and memorable than those with more points. Yet the authors acknowledge that there is no need to try to force-fit a text with two points into a three-point sermon. Rather, preachers should adapt their approach to the text they plan to preach.

Make sure to read the chapter on topical preaching, even if you are committed (like I am) to expository preaching through books and blocks of Scripture. It will explain the various fallacies we can succumb to in our interpretation of Scripture. The cautions it offers in regard to topical preaching apply to expository preaching as well. Besides, a good topical sermon is simply systematic theology for the church. So you might have an occasion to use this primer on preparing a topical sermon.

It is also apparent that Drs. Johnson and Woolsey understand how to preach faithfully to younger generations who bring a unique set of expectations and objections. The chapter on interactive talks will help preachers connect with those who want to have a conversation, while the chapter on narrative sermons will tap into the younger generation's love for stories. Don't skip the chapter on the need for a clear purpose. This is where many sermons fail when it comes to both younger and older generations. A clear purpose provides the filter for what we include in our sermon and what we leave on the cutting-room floor. It also influences the shape our sermons take and the way in which we apply them to our listeners' lives.

Finally, I am grateful for the emphasis on transformational preaching—that which first changes the preacher's life and then the lives of the hearers. When we read Scripture, we can never allow sermon preparation (What am I going to preach?) to eclipse transformation

(Who am I going to be?). As the authors observe, we change people's lives by first changing our own.

This is a terrific book – but don't just take my word for it. Take it up and read. Then go preach!

– Steven D. Mathewson
Executive Director, The Biblical Preaching Advance
Author of *The Art of Preaching Old Testament Narrative*
Author of *The Art of Preaching Old Testament Poetry*

Introduction

Everyone who hears you preach is trusting you to interpret God's Word and help them apply its meaning to their lives. The Word of God is *living and active* (Hebrews 4:12), *reviving the soul* and *rejoicing the heart* (Psalm 19:7-8), and your hearers are counting on you to show them how to make sense of their lives as they grow in godliness. We should never take this responsibility lightly.

How do we write transformational sermons that *cut to the heart* (Acts 2:37)? How do we inspire our hearers to take action and to become doers of the Word (James 1:22)? How do we point them to Christ as the solution to any problem or challenge we face?

This book is designed to arm both novice and seasoned preachers with the tools to write relevant, action-promoting sermons that speak to the heart.

Words hold power to stir hearts and ignite change. In this comprehensive guide, we embark on a journey of preparing sermons that not only captivate minds but also inspire meaningful action. In Part 1, you will learn how to preach five types of sermons: three-point expository, topical, narrative, Bible-story, and interactive talks. The methods vary within these approaches, but because the message of the gospel is the foundation for every sermon that resonates deep within the soul, the gospel must be the focus of every sermon you create. You will learn to preach about the work of Christ as the direct solution to any difficulty or problem we face in life.

Part 2 breaks down key priorities that should never be overlooked as you develop sermons. You will learn to develop a clear purpose for each sermon you write so that your audience understands the objectives of your message. You'll also learn the importance of being under divine influence while you prepare sermons and preach them. Most importantly, you'll learn how an effective preaching ministry grows out of a life that is fully surrendered to Christ.

Finally, we provide several practical resources to guide you through the sermon-preparation process, including a quick-start guide for writing three-point sermons, a sermon outline worksheet, a guide for using the "Interpretative Journey" to help you uncover what the biblical text meant to the original audience, and one hundred Bible stories that can be developed into Bible-story sermons.

May God bless you in your mission to rightly handle *the word of truth* (2 Timothy 2:15) and to help your hearers become doers!

Part 1

Building Five Styles
of Sermons

Chapter 1

How to Create Three-Point Expository Sermons

When you hear the word "sermon," what is the first thing you think of? We asked many people this question and received a variety of responses. The most common reply was "preaching," which was more encouraging than the answer given by several others: "boring."

Other replies included "hellfire," "punishment," or some other negative connotation. One person said that when he heard the word "sermon," he thought about the running back who played for both the Oklahoma Sooners and the Ohio State Buckeyes. He said, "The name of the Sooners' running back was Trey Sermon, and the funny thing is, his dad is actually a pastor."

Unfortunately, the word "sermon" doesn't usually conjure up thoughts of jubilation. Think about it. Our admittedly unscientific survey promoted *zero* enthusiastic responses. We even received a reference to a college football player, but we didn't receive a single reply that put sermons in a particularly cheerful light. No one we asked associated "sermon" with "exciting," "powerful," or "I can't wait until Sunday!"

Let's face it. We've all sat through – and maybe even preached – sermons that produced heavy eyes and stifled yawns. New preachers and seasoned veterans often struggle with basic homiletical dynamics. They may know God's Word inside and out, but their sermons lack organization, flow, and passion.

In this chapter, we will walk you through a simple yet effective approach to building a sermon that will speak to the hearts of your hearers and maybe even instill positive thoughts about the word "sermon." The sermon we will build is a three-point expository sermon. The approach we will use consists of seven steps:

Step 1: Select Your Text
Step 2: Study the Text
Step 3: Determine the Big Idea
Step 4: Identify Your Points
Step 5: Develop Your Points
Step 6: Write Your Introduction
Step 7: Write Your Closing

Step 1: Select Your Text

Most preachers write *topical* sermons. They approach their sermons by selecting and developing a topic. In this chapter, we will develop a three-point *expository* sermon, which calls for a completely different approach to creating a sermon. Expository preaching is the faithful exposition of God's Word. The preacher doesn't pick a topic and then go hunting for verses to support the topic; rather, he seeks to draw out biblical truth from a passage of Scripture in its original context.

A "text" can be any portion of Scripture, from part of a verse to an entire passage. Such passages are easy to detect if you use a study Bible, which typically divides Scripture into sections that are denoted by headings. In the ESV Study Bible, for example, Philippians 4:10-20 is titled "God's Provision." This section is a passage of Scripture that centers on a theme/thought. When deciding on a text, it is helpful to choose from an area of Scripture that you have already been reading as a part of your daily quiet time with the Lord. Be sure that the passage speaks to you personally before you present it to others. Others will be convinced of the truthfulness and applicability of the text if it has already impacted you.

The expository approach differs greatly from topical sermons. In topical messages, preachers normally make a claim and then bounce from verse to verse throughout the Bible, using such verses to prove or back up what they are saying (this is known as proof-texting).

Topical preaching can be done well if the preacher performs "mini-expositions" on the texts he uses and carefully builds these texts around a central theme. But unfortunately, unskilled and busy preachers arm themselves with a concordance, hop from verse to verse, and force-fit those verses into the message at the expense of the context. They then often read their own biases into Scripture without considering the intended message of those verses. This is called *eisegesis*, and it is simply bad preaching that leads to faulty doctrine.

In expository preaching, you select the text and let the text speak for itself. In later steps, you will mine God's Word and extract meaning from your text so that you can show your hearers how it applies to their lives.

Step 2: Study the Text

The work you do in this step is called *exegesis*, which is the task of discovering a biblical author's intended meaning for his original audience. You will examine your selected text in its historical and written context. As you study the text, think of yourself as a time traveler, and get into the shoes (or sandals) of the author. In a broad sense, you will consider the author's intended meaning and your response to the text.

Your time-travel experience also includes an investigation of the cultural, political, geographic, and religious setting of the text. Biblical commentaries, concordances, Bible dictionaries, Bible handbooks, and study Bibles will help you uncover details about the historical backdrop of your passage of Scripture. As you study the text, always pay attention to what the Holy Spirit is revealing to you.

Examining the immediate and broader context of a passage allows you to see how the text fits into the chapter, how the chapter fits into the biblical book, and how the biblical book fits into the Bible as a whole.

Looking at the biblical text within its wider framework is like considering a chapter from a novel within the wider framework of its entire story. It would be difficult to extract meaning by merely reading an isolated chapter in the middle of a book.

For example, if you merely read one chapter from a C. S. Lewis novel without reading anything before or after it in the book, you would most likely be unable to understand the chapter. You might learn about the characters, but the plot or subplot would be hard to decipher because you wouldn't know what came before. If you're unable to see how the chapter fits into the entire story, you will not understand the chapter.

Spend time exegeting the passage. Read the text several times. Use various translations to see how different translations deal with certain words and phrases. Ask the Holy Spirit for understanding. John Piper underscores the value of meditation and reflection during the exegesis process: "Take two hours to ask ten questions of Galatians 2:20, and you will gain one hundred times the insight you would have attained by quickly reading thirty pages of the New Testament or any other book. Slow down. Query. Ponder. Chew."[1]

We give a thorough treatment to studying a text in "Prepping for a Sermon or Bible Study" (Resource 1). We highly recommend that you read this resource and use the steps of the "Interpretive Journey" to prepare for your sermon.

---

[1]   John Piper, Brothers, We Are Not Professionals (Nashville: B&H Publishing Group, 2013), 94.

Step 3: Determine the Big Idea

If you were to ask the average parishioner a few hours after a church service what the pastor spoke about, many responses would begin with "Umm" as they search their memories to find any lingering remains from a message they heard just hours before. Many church attendees do not know what a preacher's sermon is about because the preacher himself does not know. He may have a clever title for his message, but that isn't enough. A sermon must have a clear, simple, central idea if everyone is to know what the sermon is about. "Oh, Mercy Me!" may be a clever title for a sermon about God's mercy, but if the message isn't cohesive with a clearly presented subject, the title may as well be "You Will Forget This Sermon by Monday."

Haddon Robinson, whose "Big Idea" preaching has influenced thousands of expository preachers, likens sermons to ammunition: "A sermon should be a bullet, not buckshot." He tells a memorable story about our thirtieth president and the ineffectiveness of the president's pastor: "Years ago, Calvin Coolidge returned from church one Sunday and was asked by his wife what the minister had talked about. Coolidge replied, 'Sin.' When his wife pressed him about what the preacher had said about sin, Coolidge responded, 'I think he was against it.'"[2]

After you have studied your selected passage for meaning and understanding (Step 2), you are ready to

---

2   Haddon Robinson, Biblical Preaching: The Development and Delivery of Expository Messages, 3rd ed. (Grand Rapids: Baker Academic, 2014), 16-17.

uncover the Big Idea. This is the most crucial step in the sermon development process. Not only does the Big Idea bring clarity and focus to your message, but your sermon points should be designed to support the Big Idea.

What Is the "Big Idea"?

The Big Idea is the single, all-encompassing concept of your sermon – the one major idea. The points of your sermon are built around this one grand thought, and everything you say in the three points that you develop must support this single main idea. This grand thought will serve as the theme of the sermon. The Big Idea is a statement from which your whole sermon emerges.

The Big Idea consists of two elements: a subject and a complement. In homiletics, the subject is a precise answer to the question "What am I talking about?" The complement completes the subject by answering the question "What am I saying about what I am talking about?"

The complement may seem confusing at first. Think of the subject as a question and the complement as the answer to that question. For example:

> **Passage of Scripture:** James 1:2-12
> **Subject:** Why should we count it all joy when our faith is tested?
> **Complement:** Because trials make us complete and whole.
> **Big Idea:** We can rejoice in trials because tested faith in Christ makes us complete and whole.

> **Passage of Scripture:** Philippians 4:10-20
> **Subject:** Why should we be content in every situation we face?
> **Complement:** Because we can trust Christ to strengthen us.
> **Big Idea:** We can be content in all situations by relying on Christ's power to strengthen us.

Don't stress yourself by looking for the "right" Big Idea – it can vary according to your audience or situation. You can draw out a minor theme from a biblical passage if there is sufficient exegetical material in the text to support the theme. Some passages may have evidence to support several Big Ideas. Two different preachers will most likely find two different Big Ideas for the same passage of Scripture. The key is to narrow in on what your audience ought to know and what God has laid upon your heart.

The Big Idea must be crystal clear to your audience. If they are asked what your sermon is about, they will be able to easily restate your Big Idea – if it is clear. Unless our ideas are expressed in words, we cannot understand or communicate them. If we cannot think ourselves clear so that we say what we mean, we have more work to do before standing behind the pulpit.

One final note regarding the Big Idea: Having a Big Idea doesn't necessarily mean you have a good idea. Run your Big Idea past others before you invest hours developing a bad idea. Once you have established your Big Idea, you're ready to develop your points.

Step 4: Identify Your Points

Next, make several observations about your Big Idea in the context of your passage. You might have five or more observations from a passage. From those observations, narrow them down to three points.

Here are five observations from Philippians 4:10-20.

> **Big Idea:** We can be content in all situations by relying on Christ's power to strengthen us.
>
> **Observation 1:** Paul experienced extreme poverty (v. 12), but was never defeated by such hardships.
>
> **Observation 2:** Paul experienced great abundance (v. 12), but was never distracted by his prosperity.
>
> **Observation 3:** Paul experienced the secret of contentment regardless of the situation: Christ's power and strength (v. 13).
>
> **Observation 4:** God met Paul's needs through others (v. 16).
>
> **Observation 5:** God met all of Paul's needs through the riches of Christ's glory (v. 19).

There are many other observations that can be made from this passage, but these five observations keep the message focused on the Big Idea you intend to use that we can be content in all situations by relying on Christ's power to strengthen us.

The job now is to narrow the observations down to

three points. Why three? If you use more than three points, you will overwhelm your audience. Three tends to be manageable and more memorable.

When you formulate your three points, consider the needs of your hearers and the situation(s) they may be facing. If your points don't relate to real life, the sermon will not be memorable or make an impact on people's lives.

A good point is derived from observations, is personalized to the audience, and is action-oriented – something the hearer can do, feel, or be. For example, Observation 1 is a good observation, but *not* a good point:

Observation: Paul experienced extreme poverty.

We must turn this observation into an action-oriented statement for it to be meaningful and applicable. Paul experienced extreme poverty, but was never defeated by his hardships. So the point we need to make should give some type of action, something to do, feel, change, etc. For example:

Point: Don't be defeated by your hardships.

With the five observations made from Philippians 4:10-20, you could develop three points to give your hearers clear actions to take:

Big Idea: We can be content in all situations by relying on Christ's power to strengthen us.

Point 1: I won't be defeated by my hardships (v. 12).

Point 2: I won't be distracted by my abundance (v. 12).

Point 3: I will be dependent on my Savior (vv. 13, 19).

Notice that the points follow a cadence: I (won't, won't, will) be (defeated, distracted, dependent) by my (hardships, abundance, Savior).

If we were to create an accompanying sermon note sheet, which is designed to encourage listener engagement, we would give our listeners an opportunity to write down the actions they must take in order to be content in all situations. The fill-in-the-blank note sheet accents the cadence that was created:

I won't be _____ by my hardships (v. 12).

I won't be _____ by my abundance (v. 12).

I will be _____ on my Savior (vv. 13, 19).

Also notice that the three key actions are alliterated: defeated, distracted, dependent. It isn't necessary to use alliteration (all three words start with "d" and even share three syllables), but it gives your points a poetic feel – and it's fun to create, facilitating the audience's remembrance of your message. See "Resource 2: Sample Big Ideas and Sermon Outlines" to see other Big Idea examples.

Once you have developed your Big Idea (Step 3) and identified your points (Step 4), you are ready for the next step.

Step 5: Develop Your Points

You will draw content from your exegesis (Step 2) to help develop your points. For each point, we use EAR – Explain, Anticipate, Relate – as supporting material:

Explain the point.

Anticipate arguments: questions, objections, doubts.

Relate the point through illustrations and application.

At first, you will most likely develop your points sequentially in the E-A-R order. As you grow in your sermon writing, however, these three elements will be smoothly interwoven and not necessarily in the E-A-R sequence. For example, you might present a point and move directly into an illustration (R) before you explain your point (E).

Explain the Point

There are at least five ways to explain each point.

Describe the situation/context of your selected passage. Point 1 of the sample sermon above is "I won't be defeated by my hardships." Explain the hardships Paul faced in his life, emphasizing how he knew what it was like to be in need or want.

Use examples to explain your point. Describe some

of the situations Paul faced that were difficult to endure (e.g., 1 Corinthians 4:11-13; 2 Corinthians 4:8-9; 6:4-10).

Explain your point by describing the individuals and events named in your passage, discussing who did what to whom and with what effect. This is called narration. In Point 3 ("I will be dependent on my Savior"), you might describe the Philippian church and how God met Paul's needs through the sacrifice of the church members. You could, perhaps, describe their characteristics: sharing (v. 14), giving (v. 18), and generosity (vv. 16-18).

Provide factual information, such as statistics. To explain Point 1 in our sample sermon, you would relay any facts to support the point. For example, "According to a recent study by the XYZ Research Group, 65 percent of all Americans facing hardships self-medicate through alcohol, prescription or illegal drugs, or pornography usage."

Quote experts. Quotations will bolster your sermon points if used well. A key reason to use quotations, according to preaching expert Haddon Robinson, is to gain authority. There are others who are more qualified to speak on certain topics (such as Haddon Robinson) than we are. We "quote others because they are in a better position to know the facts or interpret them, or because the audience would be more likely to accept their evaluation."[3] Quotes will help you explain concepts, but use them sparingly and keep them brief.

Don't use all five of the aforementioned explanation techniques for every point, but sprinkle all five throughout your points to help you explain them. Variety will help keep your sermon interesting.

---

3   Robinson, Biblical Preaching, 103.

Anticipate Arguments

As you develop each point, keep in mind that your hearers may doubt the veracity of what you're teaching. For example, the second point of our sample sermon is "I won't be distracted by my abundance." Some of your listeners might be thinking, "How can I be distracted by my abundance? Things are finally working out for me, and I'm finally happy!"

When you are fleshing out your points, ask whether your audience will accept your statement as true. If not, why not? Write down potential questions, objections, and doubts they may have. Then answer them. You might even say in your sermon, "Some of you may be thinking that . . ." or "How could it be that . . .?" Engage doubters and address their questions – even before they ask them. Show listeners that you are aware that they may take issue with your point.

The apostle Paul was a master at this, especially in the book of Romans, where he asks and answers the questions he figures his audience may contrive as they read through the points he presents (e.g., Romans 3:1-9; 6:15; 7:7). Keeping your listeners' potential objections in mind will help you present biblical truth clearly.

Relate the Point Through
Illustrations and Application

Illustrations serve a vital purpose: Well chosen, skill-fully used illustrations can do just about everything – restate, explain, validate, or apply ideas by relating them to tangible experiences. Illustrations make the truth believable to your listeners and hold their interest. Use at least one illustration for each point you develop.

There are many types of illustrations you can utilize. Personal stories always capture an audience's attention. If you tell a personal story, however, keep it modest – don't give personal stories in which you always emerge as the hero. In fact, the use of transparent vulnerability lends to the speaker's authenticity and trustworthiness. The audience will relate and identify more strongly to your humility than to your heroism. If your illustration needs a hero, make Jesus the one who shines.

You might show your audience movie clips or audio clips in which you play part of a song that is relevant to the point you are making. Live skits also work well, as do object lessons with props. You can even bring in a guest who has an experience relevant to the Big Idea of your message and interview him or her in front of the church. Be creative.

As you develop your point, think through areas that need to be illustrated for your hearers to grasp and apply the message to their lives.

In Point 1 ("I won't be defeated by my hardships"), for example, you might tell the story of Job and how he wanted to give up but didn't. Or you might tell how a friend and his wife endured her cancer diagnosis, treatment, recovery, remission, and then recurrence – all with a positive outlook. Whatever illustration(s) you choose to use, you must relate the biblical concept (the point) to your hearers in a way that ministers to their hearts and is applicable to their lives.

Application is where the rubber meets the road. Without it, your sermon has little potential to transform the lives of your listeners. Give your listeners both biblical truth and a life-shaping way to apply it.

Ask two essential questions as you develop each point:

1. **What real difference does this biblical truth make to *me*?** If God's Word is going to transform others, it must transform you first. Personal transformation is at the very core of transformational preaching. Your sermon must flow from a heart that has seen great truths in God's Word and has applied these truths. If you haven't been moved and convicted, why would you expect that effect on your audience?

2. **What real difference does this biblical truth make to my listeners?** Your listeners are looking to be fed spiritually and are hoping that you will teach them something from God's Word that is inspirational and useful for their everyday lives. In our sample sermon's first point ("I won't be defeated by my hardships"), you might ask a simple, pointed question to speak directly to your hearers: "How many of you are in a situation at home, or at work, or even at church that is causing you to grow discouraged – or even beyond discouragement?"

Explain how God will give us the strength to prevent hardships from robbing us of our peace and joy. Like Paul, we can face severe hardships and still persevere.

Don't tell them entirely "how" to endure just yet; that's coming in Point 3. For now, just make the case that God will help us have a positive outlook even in the worst situations.

That's how you could apply Point 1. You will also need to apply Points 2 and 3. For example, you might apply the third point ("I will be dependent on my Savior") by focusing on what prevents us from depending on God, emphasizing that Jesus depended on God and is our perfect example. You might stress how it is only through dependence on Christ that we can find contentment in every situation. What must we do? Change the object of our trust, or on what/whom we depend. You might say, "If I depend upon my wife for my complete satisfaction and to meet all my needs, I will certainly be disappointed, and I am not being fair to her. She's not God. My wife isn't responsible for my contentment, and true contentment can only be reached through faith in Christ Jesus. It is through Him that I can find joy and peace, knowing that the power He gives is sufficient to face every challenge."

Once you have fleshed out each of your sermon's points by explaining, anticipating arguments, and relating biblical truth through illustrations and application, you are ready to write your introduction (Step 6) and closing (Step 7).

Step 6: Write Your Introduction

Now that you know what your sermon is about, it's time to determine how you will introduce it in a way that captures the interest of your audience. In the introduction, you will present the problem in your audience's cultural context. What is the problem that you and your listeners are facing?

Address the following five areas in your introduction:

- Present the problem (e.g., "This is what we face.").

- Illustrate the problem.

- Present your sermon text and how it addresses the problem.

- Read the sermon text (your passage of Scripture).

- Present the Big Idea and pray.

Here's how you might address these five areas in our sample sermon:

Present the problem: There are many things that distract us from living a joyful life.

Illustrate the problem by saying, "I'm going to play you an audio clip from someone. Tell me – do you think this guy is content?" Then immediately play a thirty-second audio clip of the Rolling Stones' "I Can't Get No Satisfaction." Then say, "As Mick Jagger immortalized in this song, the human condition is dissatisfied."

Present your sermon text and invite your hearers to turn to Philippians 4:10. As they are turning to the text, give them some background information about the text and tell them why it was written and how it speaks to the human condition.

Read the text (Philippians 4:10-20).

State the Big Idea: "You can be content in all situations by relying on Christ's power to strengthen you. Before we break down this biblical truth, look at the scale on your note sheet." Then draw their attention to the scale created on their handout, which allows them to rate their contentment level on a scale from 1 to 10 regarding their most recent hardship. Then say, "Think about a recent hardship, trial, or challenge. On a scale from 1 to 10, circle your level of contentment during this hardship."

1	2	3	4	5	6	7	8	9	10
Barely Surviving				Utter Discontent				Pure Joy	

After inviting them to rate their contentment level, restate the Big Idea: "You can be content in all situations by relying on Christ's power to strengthen you. Today we'll see how the Bible says to do that." Then pray, inviting the Holy Spirit to encourage, challenge, and transform all of you into the image of Christ.

Your goal in the introduction is to present the subject of your sermon in a way that arouses your hearers' interest and tells them that your message is relevant to their lives. Not everyone is as giddy as you may be for your sermon to begin. In fact, some may be a little bored, and they may worry that you're about to make matters worse.

Surprise them. Make matters better. Capture their attention by causing them to smile, laugh, and think. A well-planned introduction is vital for your sermon's success.

Step 7: Write Your Closing

When you preach to transform the lives of your hearers, the closing is the most critical part of your sermon. You have answered the question "What difference does this make" throughout your message, and now it's time to ask a new question: "Are you willing to allow God to make that difference?"

The goal of your closing is to help your listeners know how to live out the truth of Sunday morning's sermon on Monday. There are four key elements to include in your closing:

1. Restate the Big Idea and review the most important assertions.

2. Illustrate with an anecdote or story that nails the truth in your listeners' minds.

3. Ask for a response. Don't merely state the facts and sit down. Good preaching asks people to respond to God's Word. One way to ask for a response is to pose a pointed question. For example, "The question of questions for all of us is . . ." or "Are you willing this morning to . . ." or "Write down in the space provided . . ."

4. Pray. Don't pray a prayer of summary. Don't teach a new lesson in your prayer or raise a new topic. Instead, ask God to work in your life and in the lives of your hearers to be transformed by Christ's power.

In our running sermon example, your closing might look like this:

1. **Review** Paul's secret for being content, mention that contentment isn't natural, but is learned (Philippians 4:12), and restate the Big Idea.

2. **Illustrate** by telling a heartwarming story of a Christmas in which a couple had little money to purchase gifts for their children, yet found a way to experience an amazing Christmas together (this is just an example; insert your own appropriate closing illustration that fits your message).

3. Ask for a **response** by inviting the congregation to think about three situations in which they need God's strength. Include a call to action on the sermon note sheet:

   Three situations for which I will rely on Christ's power to strengthen me:

   1. _____
   2. _____
   3. _____

Then say to the audience, "Mick Jagger can't find any contentment. He tries and tries and tries, but he simply "can't get no satisfaction." (Pause) Can you? Can you find satisfaction by trusting in Christ's power to strengthen you, no matter what you may be facing? Let me ask an even deeper question. (Pause) *Will* you? Will you allow Christ to strengthen you for every difficult situation you're facing?"

4. **Pray** for God's help to live by faith in Christ, in His power and strength. Ask God to work in your life so that you can become more and more like Christ, who always depended on His Father and was never disappointed.

These seven steps will help you prepare messages that are faithful to God's Word and relevant to your hearers. Remain committed to being a conduit of life transformation through the words you speak. As you do so, God will use you as He breathes life and hope into your hearers' hearts.

We have provided "A Quick Guide for Preaching a Three-Point Sermon" (Resource 3) at the back of this book as a reference tool to help you develop your sermon. Also, we invite you to reproduce "Outline Your Sermon" (Resource 4) and use it to help you outline each component of your sermon.

Final Thoughts

It is good to preach various styles of sermons, including verse-by-verse expositions, proper topical expositions, and narrative sermons. But never give up on the Big

Idea. Regardless of the style of message you preach, your hearers need to clearly know what your sermon is about.

Use application throughout your sermon, but never say, "I know what you're feeling" or "I know what you're thinking." You don't know what your listeners are feeling or thinking. Instead, say, "You may be feeling . . ." or "You might be thinking . . ."

Use inflection, varied gestures, pauses, silence, quiet tones, and loud tones to enhance your delivery. When appropriate, use intensity to show that you believe and are gripped by the truth of what you say.

Consider the valuable truths found in your regular study of God's Word. Sermons should be birthed from your regular study of Scripture and the spiritual truths you have experienced yourself. If you keep a notebook or journal of your daily study thoughts, you'll have a set of material from which to work when the need/ opportunity to preach arises.

Learn to enjoy writing sermons. In his late eighties, long after he had retired from his pastorate, my father, Howard C. Johnson, penned sermons he would never preach. Throughout his lifelong ministry, he had learned to write sermons as a devotional tool to grow in the likeness of Christ. He enjoyed going into his home office, poring over Scripture, and determining how he would present a text to an audience. Don't think of sermon writing as a tedious chore – it is an adventure to be enjoyed.

Not every expository sermon has to contain three points. If your text has two, four, or five points naturally built into it, go with the flow and abandon the three-point format. For example, in Matthew 5:13-16 (salt and light), two points flow naturally from the text. Jesus said that believers are *the salt of the earth* (v. 13) and *the light of the world* (v. 14). This text easily lends itself to a two-point sermon:

1. We are called to be salt (v. 13).

2. We are called to be light (v. 14).

A more action-oriented approach could be:

1. Season others with something precious (v. 13).

2. Be a testimony to those in darkness (v. 14).

There is no need to try and force-fit these two points into a three-point sermon. Remember, a three-point sermon is simply a way to organize your thoughts to help you preach a text so your hearers can understand and apply it.

Believe your message. If you are not convinced about what you're preaching, your audience will immediately see that and respond in kind. Why should they believe what you don't? Have passion and conviction about whatever truth you hope to convey. Be sincere and honest. You must win your audience to yourself before you win them to your message.

Focus on pleasing God, not on being amazing. Your responsibility is to be faithful and humble in handling the Word of God, while keeping in mind the burden you should have for the souls of your audience. Your sermon isn't an outlet for your ego or an opportunity for accolades. It isn't an academic presentation or an oratory performance. It is an opportunity to reveal and convey scriptural truth while feeding people with Christ. Not every sermon you preach will be presented the same or will affect everyone equally, but a consistent exposition of Scripture will cultivate life transformation for your hearers. Your sermons may not be amazing, but they will be valuable if they point your hearers to the one who is amazing, the one who can truly make a difference in their lives.

Sermon Checklist

Introduction
- ☐ I presented the problem.
- ☐ I illustrated the problem.
- ☐ I related the sermon text to the problem.
- ☐ I presented the Big Idea.
- ☐ I formulated what I want to pray.

Points

1	2	3	
☐	☐	☐	I explained biblical context in various ways.
☐	☐	☐	I anticipated arguments, objections, questions, and doubts.
☐	☐	☐	I related my point through an illustration and application, answering the question, "What real difference does this biblical truth make to me and my listeners?"

Closing
- ☐ I reviewed the Big Idea and reviewed the most important assertions.
- ☐ I provided poignant illustrations to nail truth to the listeners' minds.
- ☐ I asked for a response.
- ☐ I thought through how I want to pray.

Using a Note Sheet and a Notecard

Providing a fill-in-the-blank sermon note sheet will help keep your listeners engaged. The note sheet can be inserted into the bulletin or can be distributed before you preach. If your church is tech-savvy, your note sheet can be downloaded through an app. If you preach in an environment in which you have no access to copy machines or cell phones (e.g., prisoners who minister to other inmates or pastors of small missional communities abroad), handwrite some action steps on a notecard or quarter sheet of blank paper.

The following is an example of a sermon note sheet for a church bulletin, followed by a notecard that can be used for small gatherings.

Sermon Note Sheet

Content in Christ

Text: Philippians 4:10-20

Today's theme: I will be content in all situations if I rely on Christ's power to strengthen me.

Contentment level: Think about the biggest hardship, challenge, or trial you've recently faced. On a scale from 1 to 10, circle your level of contentment:

1	2	3	4	5	6	7	8	9	10
Barely Surviving				Utter Discontent				Pure Joy	

What does God want to teach me today?

I won't be _____ by my _____ (v. 12).
• God will help me have a *positive outlook* during trials.
I won't be _____ by my _____ (v. 12).
• God will help me reevaluate my *priorities.*
I will be _____ on my _____ (vv. 13, 19).
• I must change on *who/what* I depend.

Putting God's Word into Practice
Three situations for which I will rely on Christ's power to strengthen me:
1. _____
2. _____
3. _____

A promise to declare every time I feel defeated or distracted: *I can do all things through him who strengthens me* (Philippians 4:13).

Sermon Notecard

Content in Christ

Philippians 4:10-20

1. I won't be _____

2. I won't be _____

3. I will be _____

Three situations for which I will rely on Christ's power to strengthen me:

1. _____

2. _____

3. _____

Chapter 2

How to Create Christ-Centered Topical Sermons

A Russian student preached a topical sermon for a chapel service at Trinity Evangelical Divinity School in Chicago. The seminary student introduced his message with some humor: "In Russia, we have a saying, 'You are allowed to preach a topical sermon. But only once. And after that you must repent immediately.'"[4] Everyone in the audience laughed at the joke because trained expositors are well aware of the dangers of topical preaching.

Topical preachers are notorious for taking Scripture out of context and using it to support their ideas or arguments. They'll pick a topic (e.g., fear, love, joy), thumb through their *Strong's Concordance* to find every verse on the topic, and select the verses that support their argument. Then they make their listeners chase down all of these verses: "Now turn to . . ." The problem is that the

---

4   Sam Chan, *Evangelism in a Skeptical World* (Grand Rapids: Zondervan, 2018), 189.

verses are often taken so far out of context that the biblical author's intended meaning is completely disregarded. Instead, the verses are "proof texts" to merely prop up the preacher's agenda. In contrast, in expository preaching, the biblical text sets the agenda for the preacher.

You've probably guessed by now that we are proponents of expository preaching. We believe that expository preaching is the best approach to consistently honor God's Word and its intended meaning. But if done correctly – that is, with exegetical work on each verse or passage – topical sermons can be both appropriate and effective. The purpose of this chapter is to show how to write a good, faithful-to-the-text topical sermon. But first, let's look at where topical sermons can go wrong.

Abusing God's Word

Using a concordance to find every verse on a topic can be dangerous. It leads to potential paper cuts! Okay, all kidding aside, it leads to what are known as exegetical fallacies or word-study errors.[5] Following are some of the most common errors that topical preachers make.

English-Only Fallacy

We all know that the Bible wasn't originally written in English, yet many people conduct word studies without consulting the Hebrew or Greek word. This can easily (and often does) result in misleading or incorrect conclusions.

---

5   For more on word-study fallacies, see the thorough treatment by D. A. Carson in *Exegetical Fallacies* (Grand Rapids: Baker Books, 1998).

For example, preachers often misuse the word "vision" in Proverbs 29:18. This verse reads, "Where there is no vision, the people are unrestrained" (NASB). Expositors speak of vision as it is understood in English, especially in leadership circles – the initiative a leader has to show his followers where his organization is headed.

When preachers use the modern business definition of vision, they are not using it in the way the Bible author intended, for in context, the Hebrew word for vision (*chazoun*) means revelation or prophecy. The author of the biblical text is saying that if the prophetic words of God are ignored or rejected, sin runs rampant. This verse has nothing to do with the English use of the word "vision."

I (J.A.J.) once heard a Christian leader make a scriptural case for the modern-day practice of writing vision statements. We're not against vision statements. It is important for organizations to have them. But the Christian leader said that Habakkuk 2:2 tells us to have them: *Write the vision; make it plain on tablets, so he may run who reads it.* The Christian leader said, "How will others be able to run with your vision if it is not written clearly?"

In this context in Habakkuk, "vision" refers to the prophetic message from God, not the modern-day practice of writing vision statements. At least the speaker didn't say that Habakkuk prophesied that one day we'd all be using "tablets" and laptops, because he'd be wrong – Moses was the first to have a tablet and to download information from the cloud!

Word-Count Fallacy

This error occurs when we incorrectly assume that a word means the same thing every time it occurs. But word meanings are determined by context, not by word counts.

I (B.K.W.) once heard a sermon on the topic of falling asleep. The preacher was attempting to warn us not to fall asleep spiritually. He then tried to support his point using every passage in the Bible that mentions sleep or sleeping. One passage he used was Acts 20:7-12, where a young man named Eutychus literally fell asleep and fell to his death out of a third-story window. How ironic it was that the young man's slumber was brought on by *long preaching* (Acts 20:9 KJV). The point is that this passage has nothing to do with falling asleep spiritually, and therefore detracted from the preacher's intended message and confused his hearers.

Overload Fallacy

Many words have multiple meanings. For instance, the word "key" may refer to a tool for opening a lock, a lever pressed to play a note on a piano, or an explanation or solution, just to give a few meanings. The overload fallacy is the false notion that a word will include all or some unintended meanings every time it is used.

In the parable of the talents (Matthew 25:14-27), for example, a "talent" was a sum of money (one talent is 60 minas or 75 pounds). Some preachers will use this passage to tell their listeners that they cannot bury their talents – their natural abilities. They use this passage to challenge people to volunteer or serve in ministry:

"For those who invest their talents and use them for God's glory, God says, 'Well done, good and faithful servant.'" These pastors are guilty of the overload fallacy. Several well-known television preachers commit this fallacy quite often. When you hear a statement such as "[a certain Greek word] can also be interpreted as [a completely different meaning]," beware; you may be watching an overload fallacy at work.

Time-Frame Fallacy (also called an Anachronistic Error)

The misuse of the word "talent" is also an example of the time-frame fallacy. This is when we assign a modern definition to a word and read it back into the Bible. So, since "talent" also means one's natural ability, we take this modern definition and apply it to the "talents" in the parable, which is not how the original hearers would have likely understood it.

Word-Concept Fallacy

Some topical sermons are based on concepts. The preacher studies a specific word that describes a concept. For example, he might study the word "sin" and look up every usage of this word. The problem is that other words also describe the concept of sin – words such as transgressions, iniquities, wrongs, and wrongdoings. The concept of sin is much broader than any one word, and related words should be considered in the word study.

Selective-Evidence Fallacy

This fallacy is also known as proof-texting and is quite common among topical preachers. This is when you cite Scripture to support your argument and intentionally ignore Scripture that refutes it. It's like the preacher who tells young people, "God wants you to be single, wholly devoted to Him. Paul says, *The married man is anxious about worldly things, how to please his wife, and his interests are divided* (1 Corinthians 7:32-34). Getting married will distract you from living the life God wants you to live!"

This preacher is off track, for Paul doesn't disapprove of marriage. Paul was happy to be single, and it gave him single-minded devotion to do the Lord's work. But Paul wasn't calling everyone to be single like he was (cf. 1 Corinthians 7:28, 38; Ephesians 5:22-23; 1 Timothy 4:1-4). Scripture interprets Scripture, and if you isolate one passage or verse in order to prove a point that you want to make, you've committed a serious fallacy. The selective-evidence fallacy is particularly dangerous because it deliberately ignores Scripture, whereas in other fallacies the mistakes may be unintentional.

Topical Sermons That Do Not Betray God's Word

If you preach topical sermons, careful exegesis of each verse or passage is a must. Any topical sermon that is faithful to Scripture will have to consist of several "mini expositions" of various passages. That is, if you use a passage of Scripture to support your point, it must be explained and used within its own context. By doing so, you will draw out the *true* meaning of each text rather than superimposing your own meaning on the text.

The Deep-Gospel Topical Sermon

To create a topical sermon that is faithful to Scripture, we recommend applying the "deep-gospel pattern" to your chosen topic. A topic in such a sermon is a problem we all face (e.g., loneliness, weariness, worry), yet it has a tried and true (i.e., the *only*) solution: Jesus. In the deep-gospel pattern, the gospel and the person and work of Christ are brought to bear on the problem, and Jesus is proclaimed as the unique solution to this issue, unlike anything the world has to give.[6]

We will walk you through the steps of building a gospel-focused topical sermon in this chapter using the following meta outline.

> **Introduction:** What the problem is; our contemporary cultural context: *Here's what we face.*

> **Early Points:** What the Bible says; the original readers' cultural context: *Here's what we must do.*

> **Middle points:** What prevents us; current listeners' inward heart context: *Why we can't do it.*

---

6   A little later in this chapter, we discuss Timothy Keller's "Deep Gospel Topical Sermon" and develop an outline he presents for a sermon on the power of beauty in our culture. See Timothy Keller, *Preaching: Communicating Faith in an Age of Skepticism* (New York: Viking Press, 2015), 231, 234-235.

Late Points: How Jesus fulfills the biblical theme and solves the heart issue: *How Jesus did it.*

Application: *How through faith in Jesus you should now live.*

In the deep-gospel pattern, Jesus is the focus, not us. He is the model of how to live. Any sermon that only tells listeners how they should live without putting that standard into the context of the gospel implies that it is through our own efforts that we are rescued, and therefore, we have no need of a Savior.

So rather than saying, "This is what you need to do," the preacher says, "Here's the one who did everything for you, and through faith in Him, you can live like this too!"

Here are five steps to building a topical sermon that is grounded in the gospel:

Step 1: Determine the problem: *This is what we face.*

Step 2: Unearth the Bible's solution to the problem: *This is what we must do.*

Step 3: Explain what prevents us from solving the problem: *Why we can't do it in our own power.*

Step 4: Describe how Jesus fulfills the biblical theme: *How Jesus did it.*

Step 5: Deliver the gospel as the answer to the problem: *How through faith in Jesus you should live now.*

Building a Topical Sermon Step-by-Step

Step 1: Determine the problem: *This is what we face. (The material for the sermon introduction comes from the work you do in the first step.)*

In a gospel-focused topical sermon, your topic addresses a real-life issue. Here are four questions you can ask to help you determine a topic for your sermon:

1. What problems am I personally facing?

You live in the real world too, so your own problems and issues are likely the same ones your listeners must deal with: financial stress, relationship problems, fear about the future, grief over a loved one who has died, doubt that God will answer your prayers – the list goes on and on.

You also face the same besetting sins (pride, materialism, lust, greed, dishonesty, resentment, prejudice, etc.) and the same situations (loneliness, weariness, failure, indecision, regret, betrayal, addiction, etc.) that they face.

2. What is God teaching me?

My (J.A.J.) best resource for sermon topics comes from my daily Bible reading plan. As I mention in chapter 6, I allow God to search my heart through the

"GRIP" method of journaling (God's Word, Revelation, Implementation, Prayer). After I finish reading God's Word (G), I write down what God is revealing to me (R) and how I will implement this teaching into my life (I), and then I write a prayer based on the topic (P).

The "revelation" section of these entries is a hot spot for sermon topics. God always shows me areas of my life that need to be addressed, such as an attitude that must be changed, a behavior that must be stopped, or a relationship that needs attention. If God is speaking to me about certain issues in my own life, it is reasonable to believe that others are struggling with the same issues.

3. What issues or problems are members of my congregation facing?

Keep a sensitive ear to the needs of your listeners. What causes them worry, anxiety, heartache, etc.? Don't be like the preacher who is so hung up on his own interests – "I'm so excited to talk to you today about the stones of the ephod!" – that you become insensitive to the real issues weighing on your congregation. Address topics that are relevant to their needs. See "Appendix: Preaching to the Least of These" for specific ways you can address the needs facing those who have been marginalized and ignored by society.

4. What issues are of concern in my community, state, nation, or world?

Don't ignore the issues facing the world around you. If there is a crisis in your community that people are talking about or concerned about, you would be remiss to continue your series on the "Stones of the Ephod" while ignoring the prevalent local issue. Congregational concerns should influence what pastors choose to preach.

> Preachers will be regarded as out of touch or insensitive if they press forward with their sermon programs while ignoring a community's employment dilemma, the death of a pillar of the church, a national tragedy, a local disaster, health concerns that the elderly face, or a host of similar matters of significance in the life of the church. The world should not set the agenda for our preaching, but ministry that ignores the world that a congregation confronts is a sanctimonious sham.[7]

When the Covid-19 crisis hit the world in 2020, pastors around the world rightly took the time to address the concerns of their congregations, covering such subjects as fear, worry, loss, hope, hardships, trusting in God, and God's sovereignty. The coronavirus was on everyone's mind, and attentive pastors addressed the burdens of their listeners.

Once you determine a relevant problem to address, present the problem in your sermon's introduction.

Example:

As an example of a topical sermon, we will begin now to develop a sermon on the power of beauty in our

---

7   Brian Chapell, *Christ-Centered Preaching*, 3rd ed. (Grand Rapids: Baker Academic, 2018), 45-46.

culture. This is how we would state the problem in the sermon's introduction:

Introduction: *This is what we face.*

Our society is obsessed with beauty. Have you noticed how Hollywood portrays lawyers, police officers, office workers, or just about anyone on the silver screen? They're all gorgeous – even preachers – and we all *know* that some preachers aren't the loveliest things to look at (pointing at myself).[8] (Note: You might bolster your introduction with statistics or by quoting studies regarding the power of beauty, or by presenting relevant illustrations to emphasize what we face.)

The problem is, we use beauty as a measure of our worth. From the earliest ages, children believe they lack worth and value unless they look a certain way. The power of physical beauty over us must be broken. Look at the devastation it has brought in our society and in our lives:

- It distorts women's views of themselves (leading to self-loathing and eating disorders).

- It demoralizes aging people.

- It distorts men's lives by making them reject great spouse prospects for superficial reasons and to turn to pornography.

---

8   The introduction is a good place to use self-deprecating humor or to tell self-deprecating stories. Sam Chan says that self-deprecation makes you warm empathetically to the speaker (Chan, *Evangelism*, 207). Bryan Chapell also urges us to poke fun at ourselves, but never at others: "The only one you have a right to poke fun at from the pulpit is yourself (Corollary: the only one you cannot pat on the back is yourself)." (Chapell, *Christ-Centered Preaching*, 181).

You would then need to flesh out these points with supportive material (statistics, illustrations, examples, arguments, supportive biblical texts, etc.) as appropriate.

So in Step 1, we determine the problem (*This is what we face*), and then we transition into the solution, which is our next step.

Step 2: Unearth the Bible's solution to the problem: *This is what we must do.*

(The material for the early points of your sermon comes from the work you do in this second step.)

Once you determine the problem, your exegetical work begins. You will utilize various texts that reveal the Bible's solution to the problem. To avoid word fallacies, you must carefully exegete every supporting text you use, consulting study Bibles, lexicons, Bible translations, Bible dictionaries and handbooks, and commentaries. Conducting mini expositions of various texts will help safeguard you from taking these supporting texts out of context.

Your exegetical work will help you reveal the Bible's solution to the problem. In Step 1 we presented the problem of our society's preoccupation with physical beauty (*This is what we face*). In Step 2 we tell our hearers what they must do.

Example:
Early points: *This is what we must do.*

1. Don't judge a book by its cover. True beauty resides within, and we must look for beauty in one's

inner self (1 Peter 3:4). Gentleness (1 Peter 3:4), modesty, self-control (1 Timothy 2:9), godliness, and good works (1 Peter 2:10) are the beauty treatments that make one lovely on the inside. God set the standard. He does not see as man sees: *Man looks on the outward appearance, but the LORD looks on the heart* (1 Samuel 16:7).

2. Don't let yourself be controlled by something superficial. *Charm is deceitful, and beauty is vain* (Proverbs 31:30).

That's what we must do. Sounds easy, right? But it's not. We don't live by the old adage, "Beauty is only skin deep." We are captured by beauty, and the more skin we see – all the better. Advertisers know that sex sells. So we are powerless in our natural ability to do what we must do.

Step 3: Explain what prevents us from solving the problem: *Why we can't do it.*

(The material for the middle points of your sermon comes from the work you do in this step.)

There is something that keeps us from doing what we know we should do. That something is the wickedness of the heart. In the deep-gospel pattern of sermon development, we recognize the evil inclinations of the human heart: *The heart is deceitful above all things, and desperately sick* (Jeremiah 17:9).

We recognize not only the heart's deceitfulness, but also its power. Out of the heart *flow the springs of life* (Proverbs 4:23), which comprise a person's thoughts, feelings, words, and choices. Yet every heart has dozens of proven ways to excuse, ignore, or rationalize the wickedness in which it knows it is engaging. So the heart is a mess. That's why we can't do what the Bible calls us to do.

The goal of Step 3 is to look under the surface and explain why our hearts don't allow us to do what the Bible says we must do. You don't necessarily have to come out and say, "Look, our hearts are bad." However, you should explain that we must face the grim reality that our own hearts prevent us from doing what we must do.

Example:

Notice how the heart context is addressed in our sample topical sermon.

Middle points: *Why we can't do it.*

You know quite well we won't be able to escape the power of beauty and sexual attraction in our culture. Why can't we?

1. We desire physical beauty to cover our own sense of shame and inadequacy (Genesis 3).

2. We are afraid of our mortality and death. Even evolutionary biologists agree with Christians that the drive to possess physical beauty is a desire for youth. We'll never overcome our problems through our own effort.

Of course, these two points above would need to be further developed with supportive material (illustrations, examples, arguments, supportive biblical texts, practical application, etc.) to show how we do not have the resources to solve the heart issue ourselves. We want our listeners to feel the hopelessness of the situation. However, good news is coming!

Step 4: Describe how Jesus fulfills the biblical theme: *How Jesus did it.*

(The material for the late points of your sermon comes from the work you do in this step.)

This is where your preaching should really come to life if it hasn't already. Here you get to explain how Jesus solves the heart issue for us! He died to save us from sin, guilt, condemnation, and the consequences of our failure. It doesn't matter what the problem is: Jesus is the solution.

Example:

Here is how you could describe how Jesus did this in regard to our sermon example:

Late points: *How Jesus did it.*

You know quite well we won't be able to escape the power of beauty and sexual attraction in our culture. However:

1. There was one who was beautiful in every way, yet willingly gave it up (Philippians 2:6-8).

2. He became ugly – *marred, beyond human semblance* (Isaiah 52:14) – that we might become beautiful (Isaiah 53).

These two points would need to be developed with supportive material, but hopefully you can see how Jesus is the direct solution to the problem.

Now we come to the "Now what?" portion of the sermon.

Step 5: Deliver the gospel as the answer to the problem:
How through faith in Jesus you should now live.

(The material for your closing comes from the work you do in this step.)

The solution that we give our listeners is not some exhortation to try harder or do better. We've all heard these types of challenges (and maybe even given them ourselves). In this final stage of the sermon, you will apply the truth of the gospel to your listeners' hearts, showing them how Jesus's redemptive work on the cross and faith in Him gives us the strength and power to live right.

Example:
Closing: *How through faith in Jesus you should now live.*

Only now can things change. Only the power of Jesus can work in us to free us from idolizing beauty. Only the hope that Jesus gives us will free us from the desire for youth and the fear of our own mortality and death.

These five steps will help you build a topical sermon that is faithful to the Bible and is gospel-focused. At the close of this chapter, we give you a sample sermon that is based on the deep-gospel pattern.

Final Thought

The sermon we described in this chapter is a deep-gospel pattern. We are not suggesting that this is the only way to preach a topical sermon or is the "right" approach. We do suggest, however, that if you use another approach, you show how Jesus is the answer to the problem. Every need we have in this life is met in the death and resurrection of Christ. Without Him, we are nothing.

Even the most skilled preachers have little to offer on their own. We have a multitude to feed, yet we have the homiletic equivalence of two small fish and five loaves. That will never suffice on its own. Remember, the answer to all problems presented in sermons is Jesus, and He is also the way by which your two small fish and five loaves will feed your congregation if you let Him work through you.

Topical Sermon Example

The following is a short framework for a sermon that could be developed further, depending on the needs of your audience.

Title: Content in Christ

Step 1: Determine the problem: *This is what we face.*

The nineteenth-century showman P. T. Barnum (of the Barnum and Bailey Circus) was a driven man. He was a man on a mission for fame and fortune. His story was that of rags to riches, but he was never satisfied with his success. He always wanted more. He had critics of his circus show, so to satisfy them he hired a famous opera singer – to add some class. The capstone ballad she sang, though, is ironic. The words repeat, "Never enough, never enough." The words lament, "These hands could hold the world, but it will never be enough."

Never enough. That's the cry of the human heart. Ever since Eve desired more and gave in to the temptation of the serpent, discontentment has plagued the world. We are like Barnum. It's never enough. How much is enough? "Just a little bit more" is John D. Rockefeller's famous quote. But it's never enough.

Sometimes we think, "I'll be satisfied once ___" (fill in the blank) – once I get out of debt; once I lose weight; once my husband stops drinking; once my wife takes me back; once I have contact with my daughter . . . But even if we get our "once" fulfilled, it's still not enough.

The problem is clear. We're never satisfied. We're never content. It's never enough.

Step 2: Unearth the Bible's solution to the problem: *This is what we must do.*

The Bible has a solution to our discontentment problem. We are to be content in all situations. Paul was content regardless of his circumstances. He told the Philippians, *I know how to be brought low, and I know how to abound. In any and every circumstance, I have learned the secret of facing plenty and hunger, abundance and need* (Philippians 4:12). What was his secret? His secret was putting his faith in Christ: *I can do all things through him who strengthens me* (Philippians 4:13).

We are to be content with what we have and what we own. Paul told his protégé, Timothy, that *godliness with contentment is great gain, for we brought nothing into the world, and we cannot take anything out of the world* (1 Timothy 6:6-7). He then added, *But if we have food and clothing, with these we will be content* (1 Timothy 6:8). The writer to the Hebrews emphasized the same concept: *Be content with what you have* (Hebrews 13:5). The solution to our discontentment problem is to appreciate and to be satisfied with everything God has provided for us.

We are to be content, even through hardships. James says to count it as joy when we face various trials since they are designed to produce spiritual maturity (James 1:2-4). Paul echoes the same thing, telling us to rejoice in sufferings, *knowing that suffering produces endurance, and endurance produces character, and character produces hope* (Romans 5:3-4). We can be joyful even in the worst situations, knowing that hardships produce a step-by-step transformation that makes us more like Christ. Be joyful in trials? Who does that? We should, for that is our biblical call.

Step 3: Explain what prevents us from solving the problem: *Why we can't do it in our own power.*

Content in every circumstance. Content with what we have. Content through trials. That is our call, but do we ever fall short of doing what the Bible says to do? Yes. Why? We love the world more than anything else. We sing, "I love You, Jesus, more than anything," but when the rubber hits the road, we demonstrate a devotion to a world system that is opposed to God.

John exhorts believers to reject all that is in the world, and then he describes the things that are of this world – the very things we think will bring us contentment: *Do not love the world or the things in the world. If anyone loves the world, the love of the Father is not in him. For all that is in the world—the desires of the flesh and the desires of the eyes and pride of life—is not from the Father but is from the world* (1 John 2:15-17).

Let's break down what the world offers according to John:

1. *Desires of the flesh:* This is our preoccupation of gratifying our physical desires or our sensual bodily appetites – sexual satisfaction, the pleasure of eating, always seeking an emotional high, or anything dealing with pleasing self.

2. *Desires of the eyes:* This includes craving and accumulating things that we see, bowing to the god of materialism. The eyes trigger all of the worst activities of the self.

3. *Pride of life:* This is an obsession with one's status or importance and always involves self-display and self-glory.

These things that John warns against are the very things that we long for and seek. These things may offer momentary bliss, but they never satisfy. We're always left wanting more. The bad news is that we don't have the strength or power to war against the flesh. There is no way we can beat the nature of sin (Romans 7:9-11).

We can't please God in the flesh, nor can we defeat our flesh in an effort to please God (Romans 8:6-8).

Step 4: Describe how Jesus fulfills the biblical theme: *How Jesus did it.*

Jesus was tempted to find contentment in the same things we are tempted with, but He did not and could not sin. He is truly our model of contentment.

Read Matthew 4:1-11 – the temptation of Christ. In the first two temptations, Satan provoked Jesus with the taunt, *If you are the Son of God . . .* Jesus could have used His divine power to intervene and satisfy His human needs. However, He was content to be man, fully depend on God, and fulfill the will of His Father. He was content with the limitations of man. Using His divine power for self-satisfaction would have violated His perfect contentment and dependence on God.

Then in the third temptation, the devil said, "Okay. If You want to be man, then I'll tempt You as a man. I will surrender to You all the kingdoms and powers of the world." But Jesus is content to do God's will until the end. He knew that those kingdoms would eventually be reclaimed and restored to Him, but only by way of the cross. He could not respond to the temptation appealing to human pride since *in him there is no sin* (1 John 3:5). Jesus conquered all that we long for.

- The desires of the flesh? Satan tried to entice Jesus to give in to self-satisfaction so that His physical appetites would be satisfied; but Jesus conquers self-satisfaction.

- The desires of the eyes? Satan tried to entice Jesus with earthly glory and material possessions; but Jesus conquers materialism.

- The pride of life? Jesus was tempted to use the opportunity to display His power as the Son of God in front of a crowd of onlookers at the temple court; but Jesus conquered self-glory, content to let God glorify Him at the appropriate hour rather than take the credit and glory for Himself.

Jesus was content to live in obedience to the will of His father. He is the only person unmoved by the material things of this world.

Those things in our life that we think will bring us happiness will not bring us happiness. Anyway, they don't last, and we don't need them to be content. What will fulfill our joy, though, is being obedient to the will of our heavenly Father.

In the garden of Gethsemane, where Jesus was again tempted – this time tempted to thwart His life's mission of bearing the sins of the world – Jesus said, *My Father, if it be possible, let this cup pass from me.* The cup signified Jesus's forthcoming suffering. But then Jesus said, *Nevertheless, not as I will, but as you will* (Matthew 26:39). He completed His human mission in perfect obedience to God and fully dependent on God's grace to carry Him through. He learned what it was to obey God as man, and this was culminated and completed at the cross (Philippians 2:8; Hebrews 5:8).

Step 5: Deliver the gospel as the answer to the problem: *How through faith in Jesus you should live now.*

Jesus was content to do God's will – living the life God wanted Him to live, and dying the death God wanted Him to die. Psalm 40:8 says, *I delight to do your will, O my God.* These are Christ's words. We know this verse is messianic because the writer to the Hebrews attributed these words to Jesus, and the Holy Spirit amended them appropriately, saying, *I have come to do your will* (Hebrews 10:7, 9).

Jesus was content doing the will of His Father. It wasn't easy for Jesus, and He even asked His Father if there was any way to avoid suffering. But Jesus delighted to do His Father's will. He was content to experience humanity when He could have usurped its limitations with divine power. He was content to follow His Father's will, not longing to fulfill His human desires for comfort. Ultimately, He was approved and vindicated by His Father as having pleased Him in reverent obedience (Philippians 2:9-11; Hebrews 5:7).

You and I do not have the power on our own to resist the desires of the flesh, the desires of the eyes, or the pride of life. We don't have the ability on our own to deny self, to be satisfied with what we have, or to be content in all situations. But because of who He is and what He has done, Jesus does have the power. So what do we do? Three things:

1. We put our faith in Him.

2. We look to Him to empower us to be content in any and all situations. He will enable us to say that

God's grace is sufficient for us (2 Corinthians 12:9). Jesus's redemptive work on the cross and His resurrection enable us to have His resurrection power working in us so we can resist the world's system and value Christ as our greatest treasure. Only then can we please God.

3. We resolve that Christ is enough.

At the beginning of my message, I said that sometimes we think, "I'll be satisfied once _____" (then fill in the blank). The gospel truth is that you'll only be satisfied, truly satisfied, once you realize that Christ is enough and you rely on Him to give you joy, regardless of your circumstances.

We find contentment in doing God's will – like Christ did. Jesus was content to do God's will – living the life God wanted Him to live, and dying the death God wanted Him to die. What is the life that God wants you to live? Is it to chase the material things of this world, or is it to seek the things of God? The first may give you momentary satisfaction, but seeking to know God and grow in Christ will give you unending joy regardless of the circumstances you may face.

Let's put our faith in Jesus and pray that He will give us the power and strength to resist the desires of the flesh, the desires of the eyes, and the pride of life as we seek to be obedient to His will and live the life He wants us to live.

Close with Prayer

Chapter 3

How to Create
Narrative Sermons

Pop quiz: What was the primary method Jesus used when teaching?

If you answered, "Telling stories," you are correct. When Jesus had a point to make, He made it by telling His hearers a narrative, preaching in parables and stories.

A master pedagogue, Jesus taught us to always pray and to not lose heart by telling us a story about a persistent widow (Luke 18:1-8). He taught us not to put limits on forgiveness as He spoke about an unforgiving debtor (Matthew 18:21-35). And who can forget the wayward son (Luke 15:11-32), the repentant tax collector (Luke 18:9-14), and the wise and foolish bridesmaids (Matthew 25:1-13)?

Narrative Sermons Deliver a Single Point

Renowned theologian and pastor Charles Spurgeon learned the power of storytelling when he began his ministry at age fifteen. The newly converted Spurgeon was giving a Bible lesson to younger boys. One of his young students complained, "This is very dull, teacher. Can't you pitch us a yarn?" (The expression "pitch us a yarn" means to tell a story.) Young Spurgeon acquiesced and delivered his lesson in story form. The technique worked so well that many years later Spurgeon said he began teaching through stories because he was "obliged to tell them."[9]

Narratives can be one of your most powerful sermon styles. They have a way of delivering content that cannot be done through a standard expository or topical sermon, in which the main idea is explicitly stated. The best narratives are constructed so that the hearer arrives at the speaker's Big Idea before it is ever stated outright, teaching specific concepts without even using the words for those concepts. For example, Sam Chan uses the Greek mythological story of Icarus to illustrate:

> Icarus was a strong young man. One day his father made him wings from feathers and wax. His father told him, "With these wings you can fly, but whatever you do, don't fly too close to the sun. Otherwise, the wax will melt, and you will fall to your death."

9   Austin B. Tucker, "Guiding Preachers in Development of Narrative Skills for Sermon Illustrations" (2005). *LBTS Faculty Publications and Presentations*. Paper 326. http://digitalcommons.liberty.edu/lts_fac_pubs/326.

So Icarus put on the wings, flapped his
arms, and began to fly. As he flew, he
became pleased with himself. "Look at me!
Look at me!" he thought. He kept flying
higher and higher and higher. But eventually he got too close to the sun. The wax on
his wings melted, and the feathers fell off.
With that, Icarus fell to his death.[10]

This story teaches about pride, arrogance, and hubris
without ever using these words. We learn that disobey-
ing authority figures can lead to bad consequences,
even though this concept isn't explicitly spelled out.
Listeners are able to draw the Big Idea, that pride goes
before a fall, as they encounter the story, rather than
having these conclusions explained to them.

The key is to let an idea occur to people without stating it plainly. Saying something directly is not as potent
as when you allow people to discover it for themselves.
This is not the easiest outcome to achieve, but try to tell
the story in such a way that the listeners identify with
the thoughts, motives, reactions, and rationalizations
of the biblical characters. If you do, the listeners will
simultaneously gain insight into themselves as well. The
more the hearers identify with the narrative, the more
likely they will invest attention and thought into it.

The Three-Act Structure

Most stories can be broken down into three parts: (1) a

---

10   Sam Chan, *Evangelism*, 176.

beginning, in which context is established; (2) a middle, in which some sort of goal is sought or problem is addressed; and (3) an end, which reveals the results of reaching the goal or solving the problem. This beginning, middle, and end progression is known in plays and movies as the three-act structure:

Act I: The Current Situation
Act II: The Hopeless Complication
Act III: The Life Transformation

Every compelling story contains a life established, a situation or complication that upsets the existing state of that life, and a way in which that life can be restored. Note the beginning, middle, end progression.

Think of your own narrative sermon as a three-act play, with each act serving a specific purpose. As an example of how a three-act structure works, let's look at one of Jesus's parables. We will use the parable of the workers in the vineyard, found in Matthew 20:1-16.

ACT I: The Current Situation

The first act is when the context and characters are revealed. We are exposed to "life as usual" for the characters. The hearers should find common ground with the people in the story. In this parable, we have a very common situation: a person hires workers to accomplish a task.

Specifically, a landowner has a vineyard that must be harvested, and he hires some workers in the morning, offering a denarius for their efforts. Later, the vineyard owner realizes that he requires more help, so he hires more workers throughout the day, promising to pay each "whatever is right" (v. 4). The result was that some of the workers labored all day, while others worked only an hour.

At some point, the main character(s) will encounter a problem or dilemma. Suddenly, life is knocked off balance. As the story proceeds, the plot thickens as central characters fight to restore the initial balance. In our parable, the problem is revealed when the workers are paid their wages.

ACT II: The Hopeless Complication

In the middle of the story, the character(s) will seek to accomplish a goal or solve a problem. Protagonist figures and forces struggle to restore the balance as antagonist figures and forces struggle against the restoration of balance. There can be any number of difficulties, setbacks, and outright failures along the way. These challenges will strengthen the bond that our hearers have formed between themselves and the character(s).

In our parable, the workers notice that although some of them toiled all day, they received the same wage as the workers who worked only one hour. This problem is an easy one for our hearers to identify with. After all, "equal work for equal pay" is a mantra we have all heard. More deeply, the workers appear to be addressing an issue of fundamental fairness.

Grumbling against the landowner began to spread

among the laborers. They attempt to solve the problem by protesting, *You have made them equal to us who have borne the burden of the day and the scorching heat* (v. 12).

ACT III: The Life Transformation

In the final act, the characters deal with the success or failure met in Act II. This resolution results in a changed life and (hopefully) growth for the character. The vineyard workers who selfishly complained are challenged when the landowner confronts them with some hard truths: *Did you not agree with me for a denarius?* (v. 13) and *Am I not allowed to do what I choose with what belongs to me?* (v. 15). Matthew doesn't tell us how the workers responded, but it is safe to assume they went home duly humbled.

The point of this story goes well beyond determining a fair wage for grape pickers, but Jesus masterfully left the hearer to see it. The only clue He offers is in verse 16: *The last will be first, and the first last.* His listeners heard a story about workers in a vineyard, but received a lesson about God's sovereign purpose and pleasure. Jesus illustrated that in God's sovereignty, His grace was extending to gentiles. The workers with the contract – the Israelites – were God's chosen people. But the gentiles, who did not have the promises and the covenants, would be made equal with the Jewish people through faith in Christ. Because of God's grace and generosity, the last would become first, and salvation would be made available to all.

A basic understanding of the three-act structure is essential to telling compelling stories. With this knowledge, you are on your way to forming powerful narrative sermons.

Creating a Sermon Using the Lowry Loop

There are many different approaches to narrative-sermon writing. Eugene Lowry argues that any sermon can be plotted with strong narrative qualities. He is well known for his book *The Homiletical Plot*, in which he states:

> A sermon is not a doctrinal lecture. It is an event-in-time, a narrative art form more akin to a play or novel in shape than a book. Hence, we are not engineering scientists, we are narrative artists by professional function. . . . I propose that we begin by regarding the sermon as a homiletical plot, a narrative art form, a sacred story.[11]

Lowry lays out his own five-point "Lowry Loop" for writing narrative sermons:

> Part 1: Oops! (Upset the equilibrium.) The preacher reveals that something in our lives/hearts is not as it should be.
>
> Part 2: Ugh! (Analyze the discrepancy.) At this point, the problem/challenge gets worse before a resolution is revealed. Possible human answers are shown to be dead ends.

---

11   Eugene Lowry, *The Homiletical Plot* (Louisville: Westminster John Knox Press, 2001), xx-xxi.

Part 3: Aha! (Disclosing a clue to the resolution.) Now that the preacher has shown that human answers to the problem are hopeless, the gospel is revealed.

Part 4: Whee! (Experiencing the gospel.) Here we see that God has the only answer in Christ.

Part 5: Yeah! (Anticipating the consequences.) We now see the original problem/challenge in a whole new light. The implications for life application are also laid out.

The Lowry Loop can be used when conveying a biblical story or when illustrating a biblical concept.

Creating a Sermon Using the Pixar Pitch

While there is no right or wrong way to create a narrative sermon, you may find some methods easier than others. We think the best and most clear-cut method for developing a narrative sermon is the Pixar Pitch. Pixar? As in Disney's animation studio? Yep. This is a straightforward and easy tool for constructing a well-developed story.

Pixar writers use this tool to pitch stories for possible movie development. It utilizes the three-act structure with some additional scaffolding through the use of sentence starters. It looks like this:

Act I: The Current Situation

Once upon a time . . . (Set up the context and introduce the characters.)

Every day . . . (Convey the status quo.)
Until one day . . . (Upset the status quo.)

Act II: The Hopeless Complication (The number of obstacles in Act II will vary depending on the story.)

And because of that . . . (Face an obstacle.)
And because of that . . . (another obstacle)
And because of that . . . (another obstacle)
Until finally . . . (The solution is found – Jesus.)

Act III: The Life Transformation

And since that day . . . (how things are changed)
And the moral is . . . (What do you want your hearers to learn and/or apply?)

As you can see, the framework is quite user-friendly. We only need to address each prompt to fill out the story.

As you develop a narrative sermon, be careful not to distort the truth of Scripture. We can supply contextual information to our listeners, but we cannot present as fact anything not specifically said in the biblical account. It is far better to point out when we are speculating than to inject our own ideas into the gospels.

Building a Narrative Sermon Scene by Scene

We will now build a narrative sermon based on the story of Jairus and his daughter (Matthew 9:18-26; Mark 5:21-43; Luke 8:40-56) using the Pixar Pitch.

Act I: The Current Situation

Once upon a time . . . (Set up the context and introduce the characters.)

As we begin our narrative, we introduce Jairus. We want to show that he is just like us – a human with human needs, loves, and concerns. The most effective stories develop protagonists whom the listeners care about. The more engaged the listeners are, the more invested they will be in finding a solution to the problem/challenge that is presented, and the more likely they will see how the solution applies to their own lives.

And every day . . . (Convey the status quo.)

In order to share rich, interesting, and, most importantly, accurate contextual information, consult Bible commentaries, encyclopedias, maps, and any other resource you might have. We must learn as much as we can about the life and times of the character(s) so we can answer some basic questions: Who? Where? When? and Under what conditions? We are constructing common ground between the characters and our listeners.

The Gospels tell us that Jairus was a synagogue leader. Biblical reference materials have much to say about synagogues and associated jobs therein. We can convey his responsibilities, his typical day, and the fact that his position was an elected position that carried a certain amount of prestige. We can also infer that because he worked closely with the Pharisees, he was likely expected to stand in agreement with their opposition to Jesus.

Until one day . . . (Upset the status quo.)

This part will conclude Act I by introducing tension in the narrative. Our main character will encounter a problem that must be solved. The basic dramatic circumstance is this: Someone wants something badly and is having difficulty getting it. Here is where our hearers learn that Jairus's twelve-year-old daughter has fallen ill and is near death. Jairus likely responded in ways typical for the time. Unfortunately, all of the usual treatments must not have worked, because the girl's condition got much worse. Jairus had heard about Jesus, an itinerant teacher who had healed many. He decided he must seek out this teacher in order to save his daughter's life.

ACT II: The Hopeless Complication

We have established the first part of the basic dramatic circumstance: Someone wants something badly (Jairus wants to cure his daughter's illness and prevent her death). Now we show he is having difficulty getting it. He will have several obstacles (antagonistic problems or forces).

And because of that . . . (Face an obstacle.)

Jairus's first dilemma was facing the Pharisees. We are not given information about how Jairus dealt with them, but it was surely an issue. The Bible could not be clearer about the Pharisees' disdain for Jesus. It is safe to speculate here.

And because of that . . . (another obstacle)

Next, Jairus had to deal with the throng of people surrounding Jesus. Luke's gospel tells us that the crowd was so thick and insistent that they were literally pressing against Jesus (Luke 8:45). Yet Jairus persevered. He finally reached Jesus and fell at His feet, begging for help with his daughter.

Jesus was obviously moved by Jairus's faith because He agreed to go with Jairus to his home.

And because of that . . . (another obstacle)

Just when Jairus felt his confidence soaring, another obstacle appeared. Jesus was stopped by a woman with an issue of blood. By all accounts, it appears that Jesus had abandoned His commitment to Jairus. Jairus must have felt rising anxiety with this apparent derailment, but because Jesus is always true to His word, He continued on with Jairus after speaking with the woman.

And because of that . . . (another obstacle)

Next, Jairus faces the ultimate obstacle: One of his servants appeared and told him that his daughter had died! It surely seemed that all was lost, yet Jesus Himself was unfazed. He calmed Jairus: *Do not fear, only believe* (Mark 5:36).

Until finally . . . (The solution is found – Jesus.)

Jesus and Jairus arrive at Jairus's home. The two are greeted by a commotion of people crying and wailing loudly. When Jesus assured the crowd that the girl was not dead, but was only asleep, the crowd laughed at Him (the story's tension is at maximum here). Yet Jesus uttered the healing words, *"Talitha cumi," which means, "Little girl, I say to you, arise"* (Mark 5:41). Immediately the girl got up and walked around.

Act III: A Life Transformation

Now we share the results of Acts I and II. We explore what happens as a result of Jairus's relentless pursuit of Jesus.

And since that day . . . (how things changed)

When the crowd saw Jairus's daughter alive and well, it must have stunned them to the core. No doubt the lives of Jairus and his daughter were not the only lives that changed that day.

And the moral is . . . (What do you want your hearers to learn?)

At this point in the narrative, we will gently reiterate what Jairus took from his encounter with Jesus. Most importantly, he tirelessly pursued Jesus through obstacles, even when he thought all was lost. His pursuit paid off as he heeded Jesus's advice: *Do not fear; only believe.*

To drive home an application from our narrative,

we can wrap up our sermon with a question: "In what area of your life is Jesus speaking the profound words, *Do not fear; only believe*?" We can remind our listeners that these words were not only meant for Jairus, but they were meant for you, too. Right now, Jesus wants to speak to a desperate situation that you're facing with these words of hope: *Do not fear; only believe.*

This is a good start in the development of a narrative sermon about Jairus and his daughter. It could be fleshed out further depending on how much time is set aside for the sermon and how much relevant information we find in our reference materials. Once satisfied with the narrative, it is up to the person delivering the sermon to see what notes are needed. Some pastors use bullet points to remind them what to say, while others write out the entire narrative word for word. Use whatever method works best for you.

Final Thoughts

Narrative sermons can be your most effective messages. Why? Because everyone loves a story, and stories hold the power to communicate biblical truth in ways that might get lost in traditional propositional preaching. You may even find that you're a natural storyteller, and like Jesus, you might use this as your primary teaching tool.

We close this chapter with an example of a narrative sermon using the Lowery Loop. The following is a short framework for a sermon that can be developed further, depending on the needs of your audience.

Title: He Is Willing (Matthew 8:1-4)

Act I: The Current Situation

There was a man living in Jesus's time. He was an average guy. He was part of a loving family. He had a regular job, probably as a craftsman or something in agriculture or fishing. He was Jewish and followed Jewish laws as best he could. He attended the synagogue regularly to hear the Scriptures read.

By all respects, this guy was a model Jew. He made sacrifices to God. He rested on the Sabbath. He followed all rules to remain ceremonially clean, including staying far away from those with *sara'at* – leprosy. Going near a leper not only made one ceremonially unclean, but it also created the risk of exposure to the disease. Whenever this man heard a leper shouting, "Unclean! Unclean!" he walked well clear of the social pariah.

Act II: The Hopeless Complication

One day something terrible happened. He noticed a patch of flaky whiteness on his skin. His racing heart sank. He knew what he had to do. He had to show it to the priests. They had dominion over such matters and were the only ones who could declare a person ceremonially clean. Their word on skin conditions was blunt and final.

When he reached the priest, his world changed completely. The priest took one look and declared the man's condition *sara'at* – leprosy! The man was in shock.

He tried to wrap his head around the implications, but his racing, panicked thoughts would not cooperate. In the span of less than a minute, the man went from upstanding Jew, devout family man, and productive citizen to social outcast. He would now be sent away to live outside of the camp among the other lepers.

As time progressed, he adapted to his new way of life. He wore torn garments. He didn't go anywhere near the people of his village. He did not see his family. He shouted, "Unclean! Unclean!" as he neared others. His mindset was completely changed from that of before.

He had heard stories of lepers becoming clean, but those stories were rare, and he had certainly never witnessed that sort of thing. He never expected remission from his disease.

One day he heard about an itinerant teacher named Jesus who was traveling around and miraculously healing people. The man felt a feeling he had not felt in years. He felt hope. He was determined to find this teacher and ask for healing.

When the man learned that Jesus was in the area, he set out to find Him. As he neared a mountainside, the man saw a large crowd gathered. He got as near to the crowd as he dared and as he was allowed. Sure enough, he saw this teacher named Jesus. He decided to forgo the law and go right up to this man, Jesus. After all, a healer was not liable to catch a disease, was he?

As the man reached Jesus, his emotions overtook him. The culmination of his terrible experiences as a leper welled up inside him. He felt sure that Jesus was able to heal him if He so pleased. He knelt before Jesus and implored, *Lord, if you will, you can make me clean* (Matthew 8:2).

Although only seconds had passed, it seemed like hours had gone by as he awaited a reply from Jesus. Jesus peered down at the man and touched him! Who was this man who not only speaks to lepers but touches them? Jesus said, *I will; be clean* (Matthew 8:3).

The man looked at his arms. They were indeed clean! His legs were clean! His belly was clean! Jesus redeemed him! His body was free of the horrible disease that had separated him from the life he was intended for.

The man was instructed to go see the priests and not to tell anyone of the occurrence. He did as he was instructed, but he was sure that the story would get out since the healing happened in the middle of a crowd.

Act III: The Life Transformation

The man was able to return to his family. He resumed his old life but was forever changed. He knew that the healer, Jesus, was the Savior, the Messiah, who was spoken of in the Scriptures. He knew that God had spoken truth in those ancient writings.

This man learned rather powerfully that Jesus was willing and able to help us. The man said, *If you will*, and Jesus replied, *I will*.

In what area of your life do you need Jesus's intervention?

- Is your marriage in a rough place right now?

- Have you been struggling with an addiction

that you don't think you will ever be able to break? You've tried and tried, but you keep falling flat on your face.

- Are you single and do you feel like you'll never have someone to love again?

- Are there strained or damaged relationships in your life in which you feel that there is no hope of reconciliation?

- Are you facing a health situation like the man who had a skin disease?

It really doesn't matter what your situation is. Jesus is here today. You may be wondering if He is really willing and able to help you. Jesus is speaking to us right now with the same words that He said to the leper: *I will; be clean.*

He is willing.

Let's enlarge our faith this very moment and believe that our God is willing and eager to intervene in our lives and heal us.

Close with Prayer

Chapter 4

How to Create Bible-Story Sermons

Everybody loves a story, and the Bible is filled with hundreds of the most compelling stories ever recorded. When you preach a sermon based on a Bible story, you are sure to keep your audience on the edge of their seats. Bible stories are filled with conflict and tension, featuring heroes and villains – and in the middle of it all is Jesus.

Bible-story sermons will not only captivate your audience, but, more importantly, will also help you draw out key lessons from God's Word that your hearers can immediately apply to their lives. Your hearers will learn that the issues they face in life were also faced by the characters in God's Word, and you will be able to help your listeners respond to these issues in light of the provisions that God has ordained for them in His Word.

There are many sermon types that help preachers preach the Word, such as expository sermons, topical sermons, narrative sermons, and messages that take a verse-by-verse approach. We invite you to add Bible-story sermons to your homiletic repertoire. You'll find that such sermons are highly effective, easy to prepare, and fun to preach.

The Structure of a Bible-Story Sermon

A Bible-story sermon has a basic structure. You read the Bible story and explain key historical and cultural aspects of the story. Then you make three observations from the story. Why three? As explained in chapter 1, three points are more manageable and memorable. We want our hearers to retain as much as possible, and people can recall three items in a list fairly consistently.

Here is an outline of a Bible-story sermon with suggested time guidelines:

Introduction *(3 to 5 minutes)*

- Pray.
- Set up the story.
- Introduce the story's relevance.

First Half of the Sermon Body *(10 to 12 minutes)*

- Read the story verse by verse.
- Pause between verses to explain contextual aspects of the story.

Second Half of the Sermon
Body *(10 to 12 minutes)*

- Make a transition statement.
- Present three observations.

Closing *(3 to 5 minutes)*

- Apply the story.
- Ask for a response.

Pray

(See Resource 5 for a worksheet to help you prepare a Bible-story sermon.)

The Contents of a Bible-Story Sermon

We will walk you through each component of a Bible-story sermon using a familiar story: the story of Zacchaeus (Luke 19:1-10). (See Resource 6 for a list of one hundred Bible stories you can use to create a Bible-story sermon.)

The Sermon Introduction

The introduction to your sermon should begin with prayer. Invite the Holy Spirit to speak to the hearts of your hearers. Next, you will set up the Bible story and explain the story's relevance to your hearers' lives.

For the story of Zacchaeus, it is important to note

that he was a tax collector and would have been despised by others since tax collectors were known to make themselves rich by gouging their fellow Jews. He was certainly an outcast. Being an outcast is relevant to just about everyone. People know what it's like to be cast out or excluded on some level, such as not making a team, being teased about something as a child, or being rejected even for a good reason, such as not giving in to peer pressure.

You might say, "Well, Zacchaeus *chose* to defraud the Jews! He made himself an outcast!" That is certainly a valid point to consider, but as you analyze a Bible story for a sermon, always keep the big picture in mind. Do not get mired in details that may be relevant to the story but do not change the broad message. Because the Bible is a true account and relays true stories, there will always be details that are specific, but the message and lesson are always universal. The broad lesson of Zacchaeus's story is not about making bad choices; it is about Jesus loving and saving outcasts – and this is true even for those who are outcasts because of their own bad choices.

Another important thing to remember is that your hearers may also have familiarity with being a participant in casting someone out. In your introduction, you will draw out these things and maybe even give a spoiler alert: Jesus's encounter with Zacchaeus is a poignant example of the kingdom of God bringing salvation to outcasts such as Zacchaeus, me, and you.

First Half of the Sermon Body

You will do two things in the first half of your sermon: (1) Read the story from the Bible, and (2) pause between verses to explain cultural or historical elements of the story that need explanation. Consult a Bible dictionary or a Bible handbook to learn about historical facts. In our example, our hearers may not know that the Romans sometimes employed Jews to collect taxes, and that it was common for tax collectors to overcharge, keeping the additional revenue for themselves.

If the story you are using is quite long (e.g., Noah and the flood), don't read the entire passage. Summarize key events and read the verses that are most important to the plot. The story of Zacchaeus is short – ten verses – and can be read in its entirety.

Since we will be referring to various verses relating to Zacchaeus's story, here is the account that can be used as a point of reference:

The Story of Zacchaeus – Luke 19:1-10 (ESV)

1. *[Jesus] entered Jericho and was passing through.*

2. *And behold, there was a man named Zacchaeus. He was a chief tax collector and was rich.*

3. *And he was seeking to see who Jesus was, but on account of the crowd he could not, because he was small in stature.*

4. *So he ran on ahead and climbed up into a sycamore tree to see him, for he was about to pass that way.*

5. *And when Jesus came to the place, he looked up and said to him, "Zacchaeus, hurry and come down, for I must stay at your house today."*

6. *So he hurried and came down and received him joyfully.*

7. *And when they saw it, they all grumbled, "He has gone in to be the guest of a man who is a sinner."*

8. *And Zacchaeus stood and said to the Lord, "Behold Lord, the half of my goods I give to the poor. And if I have defrauded anyone of anything, I restore it fourfold."*

9. *And Jesus said to him, "Today salvation has come to this house, since he is also a son of Abraham.*

10. *For the Son of Man came to seek and to save the lost."*

As you read this story to your audience, pause between verses to explain cultural, political, geographical, literary, and historical issues. This will help you recreate the setting of the story. Recreating this setting is a critical component of your sermon preparation and study time.

There are certain steps to take to ensure that you engage in good exegesis, which is the process of uncovering a text's intended meaning.

No matter what style of sermon you deliver, preach what the passage says, not what you want it to say. Draw truth from the biblical story. Preachers often come to the text with an agenda. There is a point they want to make that is not supported by the Bible passage. Instead, let the text set the agenda for everything you say.

In the story of Zacchaeus, you will need to pause throughout the story to clarify things for your listeners. For example, Luke 19:2 says that Zacchaeus *was a chief tax collector.* This is a significant aspect of the story for two reasons: (1) He was considered a traitor, a turncoat. He was a Jew who worked for the Romans. The Romans heavily taxed the nations under their control to finance their world empire, which impoverished Zacchaeus's fellow Jews. (2) He was considered a cheater. Everyone knew that tax collectors made themselves rich by overcharging their own people. The nerve! And to make matters worse, Zacchaeus was a *chief* tax collector; he received additional commissions from tax collectors working under him.

These two aspects are important to explain because this demonstrates how amazing Jesus's love is. In one of the observations you will make in the second half of the sermon, you will be able to emphasize the beautiful truth that Jesus loves the unlovable.

Throughout the first half of the sermon, there will be other significant things to explain. For example:

- In verse 5 we learn that Jesus knows Zacchaeus's name, revealing Christ's omniscience and His right to call whom He chooses to call.

- In verse 8 we are introduced to biblical restitution, which was a part of God's law for Israel (see Exodus 22:1; Numbers 5:7; 2 Samuel 12:6). When someone was robbed, the guilty person was required to restore four times the amount of the loss to the victim.

- In verse 8 we are also introduced to genuine repentance. Zacchaeus doesn't just give away half of his salary, but half of his goods, clearly exceeding what the law required of him. This demonstrates that true repentance is characterized by his actions.

- In verse 9 you can discuss the significance of Jesus's statement, *Today salvation has come to this house, since he also is a son of Abraham.* The crowd believed that a man like Zacchaeus would have forfeited his access to God's favor. But Jesus declared that Zacchaeus was as much of a child of Abraham as they were. What is more, because his actions demonstrated his genuine heart change, he received God's salvation.

Explaining such contextual issues will give your hearers a good understanding of the biblical story. Don't worry if you feel you aren't able to squeeze every last drop of notable information from a passage. What information you draw out will depend on the message, and every pastor will see different things, however slight.

Second Half of the Sermon Body

During your study time, determine three takeaways or three observations from the passage that are relevant to the lives of your listeners. The first thing you need to write is a good transition statement that helps you segue from your biblical story to your three observations. Here are some universal transition statements:

- "That is such a powerful story! And I want to make three observations from this story that have direct relevance for us today."

- "Don't you love that story? It's amazing! And there are several things we can notice in this story. The first is that . . ."

From the Zacchaeus account, you might say, "Zacchaeus was a little guy, but the things we learn from his story are huge! There are three things I want you to notice . . ."

After you make a transition statement, you will unpack the three observations. Here are three example observations from the Zacchaeus story:

1. **Jesus loves the unlovable.** As you discuss this truth, ask your listeners to think about one person in their life who is hard to love. It is easy for us to love nice people and those who can do things for us. It's much more difficult for us to love people who cheat us, talk badly about us, back-stab us, etc. It's also difficult to love people who are different than us or those who are despised. For example, how many people do you know who reach out to and minister to sex offenders?

2. **The unlovable crave love and acceptance.** Zacchaeus longed to be loved. Everyone hated him, and for good reason. He was a dirty, rotten

scoundrel. Can you imagine how he must have felt when this famous person named Jesus called him by name and said He wanted a relationship with him?

3. **We are to stun the unlovable with God's love.** Zacchaeus was overjoyed when Jesus called him down from the sycamore tree. During this point you can say, "That person in your life who is hard to love – that's your Zacchaeus. That's your unlovable one. Are you willing to be like Jesus and reach out to this person, stunning him with God's love?

For each observation, use the EAR method to develop content. EAR, which is described in chapter 1, stands for Explain, Anticipate, and Relate.

Explain: Explain your observation and its significance. What is special or noteworthy about your observation?

Anticipate arguments: As you develop your observation, think about the potential questions, objections, and doubts your audience may have, and then address them. You might say in your sermon, "Some of you may be thinking that there's no way that . . ." That's a way to address potential objections people may have. In our Zacchaeus example above, an anticipated objection we addressed is: "Well, Zacchaeus *chose* to defraud the Jews! He made himself an outcast!" We would bring this up in the sermon and say that what matters is that he was an outcast – it doesn't matter how he became an outcast.

Relate: Relate material to your audience through

illustrations and examples. Illustrations and examples, such as personal stories or object lessons, help to validate ideas by relating them to tangible experiences. When you relate ideas to your audience, do so in a way that is applicable to their lives. In our third observation above in the story of Zacchaeus, we state: "That person in your life who is hard to love – that's your Zacchaeus. That's your unlovable one." We are specifically connecting the story to the lives of our hearers.

Making observations is not a complicated process. As you read and study the text during your preparation and study time, look for three lessons or truths in the story. There are more than three observations that can be made in a Bible story, but limit your observations to three, which is a manageable number to present and is easy for your hearers to remember.

Here are some examples of observations that can be made from other Bible stories:

Example 1: Job is tested (Job 1)

The story about Job begins in chapter one, where Satan is allowed to destroy Job's children, servants, livestock, and home. From the Lord's conversation with Satan, we learn a great deal about the devil.

- He is accountable to God.

- He cannot see into our minds, nor does he know the future.

- God puts limitations on what Satan can do.

Example 2: Jeremiah's letter to the exiles (Jeremiah 29:1-14)

Jeremiah encourages the exiles, telling them that God has not abandoned them or forgotten His purpose for them. God teaches us that we should:

- Press on when setbacks arise.

- Pursue the welfare of the place where we have been planted.

- Prioritize God's purpose for our lives.

Example 3: Jesus raises a widow's son from the dead (Luke 7:11-17)

All hope seems lost when the widow loses her only son, her last means of support. But we learn some special things about Jesus:

- Jesus has compassion for the hurting.

- Jesus acts on His compassion.

- Jesus can bring hope out of any tragedy.

How to Glean Observations from a Bible Story

You might automatically notice insightful things from a Bible story as you read it. However, if you struggle to glean observations, there are four questions you can ask to help you unearth key insights. It is best to select one question and use it to find your three observations. Here are the four questions and example observations:

What does the story teach you about
God, Jesus, or the Holy Spirit?

In the story of the miraculous catch (John 21:1-13), for example, here are three things we observe about Jesus:

- He knows our needs (v. 5).

- His word is trustworthy (v. 6).

- He abundantly supplies our needs (vv. 6, 11).

What does the story teach you about the gospel?

When Jesus speaks to the Samaritan woman in John 4, for example, we can observe three things about the gospel in this story:

- The gospel is for every person, regardless of his/her race.

- The gospel is for every person, regardless of his/her social position.

- The gospel is for every person, regardless of his/her past sins.

What does the story teach you about
people? (This can be things such as our
character, attitudes, and responses toward
God, sin, obstacles, the world, etc.)

In the story in which Jesus heals ten men with leprosy (Luke 17:11-19), for example, we can make three observations about people:

- People have enormous needs.

- People are prone to have ungrateful spirits.

- People are made whole only through faith in Christ.

What does the story teach us about our fallen condition and our need for a Savior?

John 9 tells the story of the man born blind. Here is what we can observe about our need for a Savior from John 9:

- Without Jesus, we are blind.

- Only Jesus can heal our blindness.

- Once we can see, we are new creations.

Asking these questions will help you draw out insights and make observations that will help your hearers apply God's Word to their lives.

An Alternative to Making Observations

As an alternative to making three observations, you can ask three questions and answer them. Your structure would look something like this:

Present the story.

Ask three questions from the story.

Answer these questions.

Sam Chan used this structure when he preached on the story of the rich man and Lazarus (Luke 16:19-31). After he told the story, he made the following transitional statement: "Wow, what a story! But if you're like me, you've probably got questions that you want answered. Let's answer them now."

He then presented his questions:

- Is hell a real place?

- What did the rich man do to deserve to be in hell?

- How do I make sure I don't end up in hell?

After he presented these questions, he said, "Well, let's go back to the story to see if we can find answers to these questions."[12]

Once you wrap up your observations, it's time to close your sermon.

Closing

There are three things to do in the closing: (1) apply the story, (2) ask for a response, and (3) pray. If your sermon lacks application, you rob your hearers of the opportunity to put into practice what they learned through your teaching. What do your hearers need to do? Your closing needs to address this.

Here is a way to apply the Zacchaeus story while asking for a response:

> You may have heard the saying, "Love the sinner, but hate the sin." However, there is another saying that I want to challenge you

12   Sam Chan, *Evangelism*, 233-234.

to adopt: "Love the sinner; invite to dinner." That is what Jesus did. He developed a relationship with one of the most undesirable and unlovable people of His day. Who is God placing on your heart right now to love?

After you ask for a response, be sure to close your sermon with a prayer, asking God's help to be a conduit of His love.

Final Thoughts

The first two chapters focus on how to preach expository sermons and topical sermons. Bible-story sermons are also a great way to engage your listeners and to present biblical truth in a format that is inherently interesting – stories. More importantly, Bible-story sermons will challenge your hearers to apply God's Word to their lives and grow in Christlikeness.

Chapter 5

How to Create
Interactive Talks

"Yes!" That was the pastor's answer when I (J.A.J.) asked him if I could start a college/career ministry at our church. Although I was already quite busy overseeing the music and worship ministries for this large, multi-service church, I had noticed that attendance was growing in all groups but one: 18-25-year-olds.

"No!" That was the response of several college students when I told them our new college group would meet every Friday night at the church campus. They said the church facility was too cold, too impersonal, too stuffy, too "churchy." They were longing to build relationships with each other in an environment that was warm, friendly, cozy, and inviting for them. They were longing for something that didn't feel institutional.

"Yikes!" That was my wife's response when I asked her if she would be open to having the college group meet at our house every week. But she agreed that our house was the best place to meet, so on Friday nights, more than twenty young adults met at our home to eat, hang out, and study God's Word. It was during these gatherings that I learned to develop what is called an "interactive talk."

There is a time and place for preaching formal sermons, and I quickly learned that Friday nights in the church building would be neither the time nor the place for those.

I vividly remember our inaugural meeting. An atmosphere of excitement permeated the room – until I stepped up to teach. My sermon was well prepared and was sure to be a home run, so I thought. It was laced with interesting stories, useful illustrations, and thoughtful explanation and application. But I struck out. As I taught, I watched a bunch of bored young people squirming in their seats, whispering to each other, and waiting for me to wrap things up so they could hang out with each other. They were not opposed to studying the Bible; it was my presentation that was at fault.

Those in attendance not only wanted to ditch the stuffy church environment, but they were also hoping to dodge a stuffy sermon. They were anything but eager to listen to me give a lecture-style talk; they got plenty of that in their college classes. They wanted to interact with each other, eager to discuss how God's Word applied to their lives. In short, they wanted an opportunity to give their input, not just take my output.

The next week I changed my style of communication and began to give interactive talks, and this completely changed the dynamics of the group. An interactive talk takes the bat out of your hands and, to continue the baseball analogy, puts it into the hands of each person in attendance. They become participants rather than spectators. And did they ever hit the ball! We discussed topics ranging from the existence of God to living out their faith in practical ways.

I encouraged participation from every person, and as it turned out, not much encouragement was necessary. They were eager to talk. As we discussed a given topic, I would ask "discovery questions," and their combined insights and observations were greater than any one person's.

I also removed the perceived teacher-student hierarchy and sat among them rather than standing above them. We sat together in a circle, and this also cultivated participation.

If you are preaching to large, formal gatherings of people, then expository, topical, and Bible-story sermons can be quite effective; but smaller groups are better served through interactive talks that invite group participation.

Format of an Interactive Talk

There are several ways to format an interactive talk. The one we recommend follows an expository approach, focusing on one unit of Scripture and its application to the lives of those in attendance.

Introduction (3 to 5 minutes)

- Set up the story.

- Introduce the story's relevance.

- Pray, inviting the Holy Spirit to speak to hearts.

Read the Bible Story or Passage (5 to 10 minutes)
Simply read the text directly from the Bible.

- **Transition** (1 to 2 minutes)

- Smoothly flow from the biblical text to the discovery questions.

Interchange (20 to 25 minutes)

- Use a set of prepared questions to help participants discover the meaning of the text and its relevance to their lives.

Wrap Up (3 to 5 minutes)

- Let the group know what actions to take.

The following seven steps will walk you through the process of building an interactive talk based on the format above.

How to Build an Interactive Talk

Step 1: Select a Bible Story

We suggest you use a Bible story when giving an interactive talk. People love stories, and you will keep your group engaged by telling them a biblical story and interacting with them about it. Besides, most people are "concrete-relational learners" and relate to stories more than to abstract concepts. Four out of five people in the Western world, and nine out of ten non-Westerners, prefer concrete-relational learning.[13] But keep in mind that you can use interactive talks with any passage from God's Word.

Take the needs of your audience into consideration when selecting a Bible story. For example, if you are giving an interactive talk to a group consisting of many nonbelievers, the parables of the lost sheep, lost coin, and lost son (Luke 15) would make good choices. On the other hand, if you are meeting with mature believers, you might choose the story of Jesus's temptation (Luke 4:1-15) to help them cultivate their dependence on the Holy Spirit when they are faced with temptation.

Step 2: Study the Story

When you preach an expository sermon, you need to know everything about the context of the passage in order to rightly handle God's Word. It's no different when you're preparing to give an interactive talk. You must do your exegetical work and know everything about the biblical account. Not only will you introduce the story with relative background information, but your listeners will potentially raise questions about the story that you will need to answer.

As you prepare your talk, read various translations and consult study Bibles, commentaries, lexicons, and other exegetical resources to help you learn the context of the story, the meaning intended for the original audience, and

---

13   Sam Chan, *Evangelism*, 174-175.

its relevance for us. You may even want to bring some of these resources to your gathering and have your participants use them. They will get practice using exegetical materials, and it demonstrates that you don't pretend to have all the wisdom on your own – you use resources.

Your exegetical preparatory work should help you answer the questions that will be addressed in the introduction of your talk:

- What is the story about?

- What real-life issue (both then and now) is addressed in the story? In other words, you must be prepared to tell your listeners, "This is what we face in life."

Step 3: Prepare Your Introduction

Your introduction should be brief: three to five minutes. You will do three basic things in your introduction:

Set up the story. You will introduce elements of the story, such as the setting, the purpose, the characters, etc., and give an overview of the story. This is where your exegetical work from the previous step comes to life. You will tell the people what the story is about, but do not spoil the plot. The group will discover it together when you read the story to them.

If I were to give an interactive talk on Luke 7:11-17, the account in which Jesus raises a widow's son from the dead, I would set up the story like this:

> Today we're going to hear a story about
> a woman who lost everything. She was a

widow, which obviously means her husband had died. But if that wasn't enough, her only son also died. This was a devastating situation for her, for not only did she lose her beloved son, but she also lost her last means of support. In Bible times, it was the responsibility of the sons to care for and provide for their widowed mothers. Unless a relative stepped up to help this woman, her future would be dismal. She would likely become a beggar.

Notice that I do not reveal what happens in the story. For the setup, I'm using exegetical work (the circumstances of widows in the culture of the day) to develop one of the characters – the widow – and to give a little background of the story.

Introduce the story's relevance. Explain how the story relates to your audience's world. The Bible addresses real-life issues, and the biblical story you selected speaks to personal issues your audience is facing. It doesn't matter what story or passage of Scripture you select, for every passage of Scripture can be applied to issues your hearers are facing.

For the interactive talk on the woman who lost everything (Luke 7:11-17), I would connect her situation to those in my audience who may be facing loss, abandonment, or a trying situation:

This is a very important story for us to consider today because, like the widow, we all

face desperate situations. They might not
be as dire as hers – losing everything – or
maybe they are. We all face situations in
life – big and small – that cause concern,
worry, and even desperation.

Next, I would adjust what I say to the particular
audience that I'm addressing. For example, if I'm speaking to prisoners, I might discuss the pain of divorce or
the heartache involved with being separated from their
children and having little or no contact with them. I
might bring up the feelings of abandonment that arise
every time their mailbox is opened, only to find it empty.

Think about the heart issues of those in your audience and address those issues, but don't reveal how
God solves the problem or how He brings hope out of
tragedy. The group will discover this together as your
talk unfolds.

Pray. Invite the Holy Spirit to speak to hearts, but
don't preach a sermon in your prayer. Invite the Holy
Spirit to reveal God's truth to everyone who is gathered.

Step 4: Practice Reading the Story

In an interactive talk, you read the story from the
Bible. Practice reading the Scripture portion aloud
many times, paying attention to unfamiliar terms and
words that are hard to pronounce. Practice reading with
feeling. Your expression and inflection should vary in
conjunction with the emotions and truth of the text.
A good storyteller uses his voice and body language to
help the audience feel the emotion and drama in the

story. Practice looking up once in a while as you read. You'll want to engage the eyes of your hearers.

In the story of the desperate woman, I would slow down my rhythm and lower my voice when I read Jesus's tender words to the heartbroken widow: *Do not weep* (Luke 7:13). In the next verse, when Jesus resurrects her son, I would raise my voice a little and say with passion, *Young man, I say to you, arise* (v. 14). Then I would pause to let the gravity of the moment sink in.

God's Word is alive and active (Hebrews 4:12), and you will diminish its power if you butcher the words or read it monotonously.

Before you read the story to your audience on the day of your talk, tell them that there will be questions afterward, so encourage them to listen carefully to the story.

Step 5: Prepare the Transition

The transition is simply a one- to two-minute bridge to help you move smoothly from your biblical story to the discovery questions. Make a relevant comment about the story and then tell everyone what to expect next. For example:

> This account is another amazing story
> that reveals Jesus's love and compassion
> for those who are hurting. It's amazing,
> isn't it? I could tell you what impresses me
> about the story, but I want to hear from
> you. I've got a series of questions that
> I am going to pose, and I know that as

we interact with each other and participate together, we will gain some valuable
insights and learn some helpful lessons.

If group members are new to each other, assure them
that your setting is a safe place to talk – a judgment-
free zone (and as facilitator of the discussion, be sure
that you fulfill your promise).

Step 6: Prepare Discovery Questions

This is the heart of your presentation. You will pose
a series of questions about the biblical passage and then
facilitate discussion. You will be surprised how much
insight and knowledge arise from these discussions. In
essence, everyone is cocreating the interactive sermon
in real time.

Following are some example discovery questions that
relate to the story of the woman at the well (John 4:1-42).

- Put yourself in the woman's shoes. What
  was life like prior to meeting Jesus?

- What reservations might she have about
  meeting Jesus?

- How do you think you might have behaved
  toward her in those times?

- If you encountered a woman in this situation today, how would you respond?

- What problem was solved that only Jesus
  could solve?

- What idea or thought do you want to take with you this week?

As you develop questions, remember to keep them open-ended as much as possible. There are certainly times when yes/no questions are appropriate, but they do not encourage discussion. You may struggle with writing open-ended, stimulating questions at first, but as you practice writing them, you will find that they come more easily. You may also find it helpful to utilize some of the overarching discovery questions listed below:

- What impressed you about the story?

- How did the story make you feel?

- What questions do you want answered from the story?

- What does the story teach us about people?

- What does the story teach us about Jesus (and/or God)?

- What problem is solved that only Jesus could solve?

- What is God teaching you from this story?

Here is another set of questions that help facilitate discussion:

- What shocked or surprised you in the story?

- What don't you understand in the story?

- What would you say is the main idea in the story?

- What does the story teach you about God, Jesus, and yourself?

- What problem is solved that only Jesus could solve?

- Because of the story, how will you live differently?

If you are focusing on a passage of Scripture that is not a story, your questions will be based on the text. Here are some potential questions for you to ask:

- What did you like or appreciate about what you read?

- What didn't you like, or what bothered you?

- What was confusing or difficult to understand?

- What new thing did you learn about God?

- What problem is solved that only Jesus could solve?

- What idea or thought do you want to take with you this week?

If you are taking your audience through any of Jesus's miracles, such as "Changing Water into Wine" (John 2:1-11) or the "Feeding of the 5,000" (John 6:1-14), here are some simple questions you can ask:

- What does this passage tell us about the way people are?

- What does it tell us about what people need?

- What does it tell us about the person of Jesus?

- What problem is solved that only Jesus could solve?

- How can we apply this to our lives?

You'll notice that in each set of questions, the question "What problem is solved that only Jesus could solve?" is asked. It's very important to ask that or a similar question. It helps your group focus on how the power of the gospel in the work of Christ is the direct solution to any problem we face in life.

Also notice that in each set of questions, the final question focuses on application. Be sure to use your time wisely so that enough time is spent discussing how the Scripture can be lived out. As communicators of God's Word, we are here to help others experience the life transformation offered by the gospel.

Finally, rely on the Holy Spirit to make comments and ask questions that were unplanned. The Holy Spirit will help you ask probing follow-up questions to the responses of your participants. Your preplanned questions are important, but engaging follow-up questions will help probe the discussion.

Your wrap-up is the last thing your group will hear and hopefully remember. You might have to develop your wrap-up on the spot, depending on how the discussion unfolds. But most of the time you will be answering one central question: "What does God want my hearers to do with the lesson(s) they learned?"

You've already asked your audience what the story teaches about God, Jesus, and themselves, and you have asked them how they can apply the biblical truth to their lives. Your wrap-up will now challenge everyone to put their faith in Jesus so they can live their lives differently. You might say:

> The final question for us today is – and
> you don't have to answer this one out loud
> – "What now?" In other words, what will
> you do with what you have learned? We
> can sit on it, or we can let it shape us. We
> can ignore it and go on unaffected, or we
> can let it change us.

Then you can personalize the "what now" concept. For example, if the topic of your interactive talk is evangelism, you might ask, "Who is someone whom you regularly see whom you can bring to church this weekend?" If your topic is forgiveness, you might say, "The Lord is most likely dealing with you about someone you need to forgive. What step will you take today to forgive this person?" If your topic is about trusting God, you could ask, "What situation are you currently facing that has caused you worry, concern, or heartache?"

To emphasize the gospel in your wrap-up, Tim Keller recommends that you draw your listeners to live like

Jesus. Rather than telling them to live a certain way, tell them that they do not have the power to do so. You would say, "You can't live like this. Oh, but there's one who did! And through faith in Him you can begin to live like this too."[14] Such a statement moves the talk from being about them to being about Jesus.

Tips for Creating a Discussion-Friendly Atmosphere

There are specific ways you can encourage participation.

Stay on track. If a question or comment takes the discussion off course, suggest that it can be addressed after the meeting.

Never put anyone on the spot. Some people will not speak in a group setting; they would rather have a root canal than speak in front of others! Respect that. Don't insist that everyone must participate.

Tactfully deal with monopolizers. There's one in every crowd – the person who loves to answer every question. That is when you can say, "Let's open up this discussion a little. I wonder what others think about this."

Be humble. If someone asks a question to which you don't know the answer, say, "That's a really good question, and I don't know the answer to it. Does anybody know?" If no one knows the answer, tell the group you'll look it up and share the answer at the next meeting.

---

14   Timothy Keller, *Preaching: Communicating Faith in an Age of Skepticism* (New York: Viking Press, 2015), 179.

Final Thoughts

Early in my ministry, I experienced the power of interactive talks when ministering to college students. Since then, I have continued to see God change lives when people interact with each other around God's Word. True fellowship takes place. Everyone is involved and engaged in the talk, relationships are cultivated through these spiritual conversations, and spiritual growth takes place communally.

An interactive talk is an excellent tool for Bible-study teachers, small-group leaders, church planters, or for anyone else who leads smaller groups of people. As you hone your proficiency at facilitating interactive talks, you will no doubt find their usefulness for occasions other than church services. They are effective in leadership retreats, prayer meetings, and even staff training. Simply adhere to the overall process and structure, and then alter your presentation materials and objectives.

Part 2

Preaching Practices and Priorities

Chapter 6

Your Sermon Needs a Clear Purpose

B y the time you finish reading this chapter, you will be able to (1) write sermon objectives and (2) explain why sermons should always have objectives.

The above statement is known as an instructional objective or learning outcome. Effective communicators use them to let their listeners know the purpose of their communication.

Why exactly did the apostle Paul write his first epistle to Timothy? *I am writing these things to you so that . . . you may know how one ought to behave in the household of God* (1 Timothy 3:14-15).

What was the purpose of Jude's letter? *I found it necessary to write appealing to you to contend for the faith* (Jude 1:3).

We know the purposes of Paul and Jude because they did the obvious thing: they told us. Unfortunately, too many people leave church wondering what they were supposed to get from the sermon, what they are supposed to do with the information, and how they are supposed to do it. The pastor either expected the hearers to just "get it" or, quite possibly, the pastor didn't know either.

Having a specific purpose and application to your sermon is essential. Yes – we explain, illustrate, exhort, and exegete, but we must understand that every sermon should change lives in some specific way.

If your hearers cannot explain the purpose and application of your sermon, then you were ineffective. You may have spoken for twenty to forty minutes, but you didn't say much. This is because your message did not include a specific action-oriented purpose. There was either no takeaway, or if there was, you did not make it clear. When a shepherd intends to feed his flock, he doesn't lead them to a sparsely green field and hope they locate food. Worse yet would be to take them to fallow ground, hoping they won't notice that there is no nourishment to be found.

If you want to lead your flock to rich grassland where they can get their fill, each of your sermons must have a purpose with application, and you must share that purpose. Better yet, lead them directly into action, large or small, that applies your purpose.

Outcome-Oriented Preaching

The purpose of your sermon isn't just why you are delivering it – it is more than that. The purpose is what you intend as an outcome. What ultimately do you want your listeners to do with what you share? What outcome are you looking for? A change in attitude? A new insight?

An action? In the teaching world, this essential element is called an instructional objective. And here's the catch: it should be observable.

In the classroom, a math teacher is expected to begin with something like, "By the time this lesson is complete, you will be able to add polynomials." An intended outcome is laid out plainly. Knowing this objective is helpful for students because they know what is expected of them. Having this objective is also helpful for the teacher because he or she won't waste time on material that doesn't work toward the intended outcome. The lesson has a focus.

In the church setting, the pastor may or may not overtly state the intended outcome at the outset of the sermon, but knowing the objective will certainly give focus and purpose to the sermon.

While delivering a sermon is decidedly different from teaching algebra, both classroom students and church attendees benefit greatly from knowing what to do and how to do it. Here are some examples of sermon purposes with action outcomes.

- My listeners will know why God expects us to forgive others and will start the process of forgiveness with someone.

- My listeners will show why God expects intercessory prayer and will begin praying for others.

- My listeners will be able to describe spiritual gifts and will be able to identify their own spiritual gifts.

- My listeners will know and be able to explain the process of sanctification.

Notice that each purpose has two elements: (1) a knowledge element: We should always be illuminating the Word and explaining how it applies to us; and (2) an action element: After your listeners hear the Word, lead them into doing the Word.

James tells us to *be doers of the word, and not hearers only* (James 1:22). Effective preachers offer their hearers a method of doing the Word.

What should your hearers do? It depends on your message, of course, but in general, your message should lead to a specific action, a change in attitude, and/or an increase in aptitude about Jesus and His Word.

The chart below contains some verb phrases that can be used to engage action, change attitudes, or increase aptitudes:

Purpose	Verbs	Examples
Action	List, write, name, define, pray, plan, enroll, contact, forgive, etc.	"On the back of your program, name three people you know whom you can pray for every day for the next two weeks."
Attitude	Appreciate, think about, recognize, commit to, plan to, see the glory of, realize, have confidence in, consider, etc.	"Think about what it means to be elected by God to receive eternal life. Also, think about your many blessings." "Turn to someone and explain the meaning of grace and why receiving it is so special."
Aptitude	Identify God's purpose for, explain, describe, paraphrase, list, name, recount, find examples of, list the reasons, etc.	"The next time you study the Bible, read a few Psalms. See if you can identify passages that clearly refer to Jesus." (Your listeners don't just need to know what to do, but they also need to know how to do it. You not only have to offer them biblical insight, but you also have to offer them skills and wisdom to live out that insight.)

Below are two examples of action outcomes in a sermon's conclusion:

Example 1: Is there someone with whom you have a broken relationship – a spouse, a parent, a friend? As a follower of Jesus Christ, you need to take the first step today to make it right. Is there a letter you should write? Is there a phone call you should make? Is there a visit you should make or a conversation you should have? Will you then ask God for the courage to make that contact and take that step to get the matter settled?

Example 2: Your job is the will of God for you. Tomorrow when you go to work, take out a Post-it note and write, "God has put me here to serve Him today." Then place the note on your desk or in your locker – someplace where you can see it easily. Whenever you look at that note, breathe a prayer: "Lord, I'm working this job for You. Help me to do it to please You." In doing so, you can remember the workday to keep it holy.

Notice how the action is tied to the knowledge conveyed in the sermon. More importantly, do you see the urgency? "Take the first step today." "Tomorrow when you go to work." God doesn't want our obedience eventually. He doesn't want us to obey His Word someday. He wants and expects us to follow Him immediately. Help your hearers do that.

How is it done?

Adding outcomes to your sermons is really quite simple. If you are following the advice in this book, your sermons will have a Big Idea. It is from this Big Idea that your outcome actions will flow.

Let's look at a Big Idea. Suppose you write an expository sermon on Psalm 117. Your Big Idea may be that the Lord would be praised because first, His love is strong, and second, His love is eternal. You might have each person in your congregation start by writing down three ways God has shown His faithfulness to them. Then you can give the congregation a moment of silence during which each person can lift up a prayer of praise for those three things.

It is always a good idea to have your hearers participate overtly. This means that you can watch them take action. (Giving people a chance to move a little also keeps their attention.) Here are a few sentence starters for both overt and covert participation.

Overt (Outwardly)

- Write down three examples of . . .
- Turn to a neighbor and tell him or her . . .
- Raise your hand if you've ever wondered . . .
- Hold up your Bible and say . . .
- Place your hand over your heart and say . . .

Covert (Inwardly)

- Think about a time when you . . .
- Imagine a situation . . .
- Lift a silent prayer about . . .
- Think of three people who . . .

Apply the Biblical Principle

When you apply Scripture in your sermon, it is essential that you apply the principle that the Bible is conveying – not what you want it to convey.

Let's look at Romans 8:37: *No, in all these things we are more than conquerors through him who loved us.*

We must exegete properly in order to extract the correct application. In the case of Romans 8:37, this verse gets taken out of context quite often. Proper exegesis reveals:

1. Paul (a Christian) recounts present sufferings (Romans 8:18).

2. The trials and threats were attempts to separate Paul from God and His love.

3. Paul credits Christ for his ability to conquer these types of trials.

Many people take this verse to mean that they are more than conquerors in all things they do for any reason. While that may indeed be true, Paul was neither stating nor implying that here. He asks the question, "Can these things [tribulation, distress, persecution, famine, nakedness, danger, or sword] *separate us from the love of Christ?* (v. 35). He answers the question by telling us *No*, they cannot, but we will conquer them all through Christ (v. 37). So here are three principles we can take away:

1. A Christian ...

2. who is facing hardships that try to separate the believer from God and His love ...

3. is more than a conqueror when facing these trials. He/she will never be separated from God's love.

Strictly speaking, this verse only applies to a situation that has all three of the above principles.

So if we preach a sermon about Romans 8:37, our objective might be presented as: "Today we will discuss what Paul meant when he said that we are more than conquerors in Christ, and we will see what that looks like in our lives."

At the end of the sermon, when we invite our hearers to apply Romans 8:37, we may describe one or two scenarios in which the verse applies. We can then have our hearers think about or list some hardships they may have that challenge their trust in Christ. We can encourage them to be comforted because of God's promise that we are more than conquerors in these trials and can never be separated from Christ; we are secure in His love.

At the beginning of the chapter, we promised you that by the time you finished reading this chapter, you would be able to (1) write sermon objectives and (2) explain why sermons should always have objectives. I hope we kept our promise!

Chapter 7

Change People's Lives by First Changing Your Own

Transformational preaching is preaching that flows from the heart of one who has seen great truths in God's Word, has personally applied what he has seen, and is eager to share it with others.

I (J.A.J) feel sorry for the members of my first pastorate. They had to listen to a young, inexperienced pastor stumble over his words every Sunday. May God bless and reward them for their patience and kindness.

My first year behind the pulpit was rough. I was always dumbfounded by how brutally swift Sundays came. I loved to preach – I just didn't always know what to preach. Like many pastors, I would go hunting for topics and ideas that I felt were interesting and relevant, and then force-fit them into Scripture so that they had some semblance of biblical support.

Then a true-blue miracle happened: I discovered

"Pastors.com," Rick Warren's database of prepackaged sermons. I felt blessed by God Himself. I could buy a sermon manuscript, an accompanying fill-in-the-blank note sheet for the bulletin, and a PowerPoint presentation for about the cost of a latte.

Hallelujah! I'm sure that's what my parishioners thought to themselves, for my sermons had gone from pointless to on point – even if it was Rick Warren's point. I would still occasionally preach "original" messages, but whether I was preaching a five-dollar sermon or one of my own gems, the usual tormenting questions sullied my Monday right on schedule: "Now what? What do I preach this weekend?" And the clock began to tick.

My heart was in the right place; it just wasn't in the right condition. Then something happened that revolutionized my preaching ministry. I learned how to read. That is, I learned how to read God's Word, how to let God's Word read me, and how to read the needs of my congregation. Becoming such a reader is the springboard for transformational preaching, and it transformed me in the process. Let's break down these three ways of reading.

How to Read Your Bible

Many pastors, especially those who preach weekly, read and study the Bible for a single purpose: to prepare sermons. They don't pore over Scripture to allow God's transforming power to change their lives. Too often, "What am I going to preach?" trumps "Who am I going to be?"

When we teachers of God's Word read our Bible, our goal should be to allow God's Word to change us, not just to write good sermons.

Wayne Cordiero taught me how to read the Bible at one of his leadership practicums. He charged the attendees to make it a practice to establish a set time to read God's Word and to journal every day. He taught us a journaling technique called the SOAP method.

The journaling instructions are simple. Start with "S," which stands for "Scripture." After you read God's Word (preferably from a systematic reading plan), write down a verse that was the most meaningful to you – a verse that really stood out to you.

Then comes "O" for "Observation." Write down what you observe about the verse. What is God teaching? Why is this verse important?

Next up is "A" for "Application." How does this verse apply to your thoughts, beliefs, or actions? Is God correcting you? Is He encouraging you? Is He asking you to do something or not to do something? How can you implement this verse into your life personally? Don't think about your ministry or church now, but think about something truly personal, such as your marriage or your children.

Finally, "P" stands for "Prayer." After you apply the Scripture to your life, compose a prayer related to your observation and application. This might be a prayer of commitment, a request for help, a confession, or even a complaint. Keep it raw and real. Put on paper what is in your heart. The purpose of this type of Bible reading and reflection is transformation. You are not trying to impress God with platitudes or smooth words, but you are offering yourself up to be reshaped.

After I implemented Cordiero's approach to Bible reading, I never had to hunt for sermon topics again. God began speaking to my heart. As I journaled week after week, God's Word was transforming me, and I realized that the things I was applying to my very own life had relevance to others. Before we proclaim the message of the Bible to others, we must first live with that message ourselves. Journaling will help you do so.

Eventually, my daily journaling procedure morphed into what I call the GRIP method (God's Word, Revelation, Implementation, and Prayer), which focuses on how God is describing Himself and His will through a given passage, and how we will implement what He reveals personally and immediately to become more like Christ. Whether you use SOAP, GRIP, or another method of personal application, the underlying principle remains the same: Before you try to help others change their lives, allow God to change yours.

How God's Word Reads You

When you read God's Word, let it examine the hidden parts of your life – those secret places in the recesses of your heart that are ungodly. Lustful thoughts, selfish motives, unforgiveness, and feelings of revenge are some of the unseen iniquities that reside deep within. Be sensitive to the feelings of conviction that the Holy Spirit brings. A fitting prayer to lift for this purpose is: *Search me, O God, and know my heart! Try me and know my thoughts! And see if there be any grievous way in me, and lead me in the way everlasting!* (Psalm 139:23-24).

As you ask God to search, try, see, and lead you, He will show you, through His Word, areas of brokenness that He longs to transform into wholeness in Christ. God's Word needs to penetrate deep into our lives – underneath the surface. That is what will bear fruit in your preaching. You can't get that from a prepaid sermon, and you can't read that in a commentary.

Read the Needs of Your Congregation

The individuals in your church have real needs, and God has commissioned you to address them. Your sermon's purpose is to change people's lives, and you can only do this if you are in tune with your congregation.

It is vital to address three questions if you are going to be a preacher who meets people's needs:

What is happening in the lives of my listeners?

Pay attention to the needs and challenges of those to whom you are ministering. What are their struggles? What are they worrying about? If you are inattentive to what is taking place in your listeners' lives, you will miss opportunities to be a conduit of life transformation. Haddon Robinson wrote:

> Normal people do not lose sleep over the Jebusites, the Canaanites, or the Perizzites, even about what Abraham, Moses, or Paul has said or done. They lie awake wondering

about grocery prices, crop failures, quarrels with a spouse, diagnosis of a malignancy, a frustrating sex life, or the rat race where only rats seem to win.

Asking "What is happening in the lives of my listeners?" will help you apply biblical truth to the issues your hearers are facing.

What is happening in my own life?

You live in the same world as your listeners. Any challenge, trial, or hardship you are experiencing is probably commonplace among your congregation as well. Just like the people in your church, you encounter stress, anxiety, sadness, heartache, temptation, and prideful attitudes. Sometimes you can simply preach to yourself, knowing that your parishioners will relate to those real-life needs.

What is happening in the world?

People are affected by what is on the news. Hurricanes and mass shootings leave people feeling scared and confused. If your city or nation is facing a major crisis, your congregation will be looking to you to help them make sense of it. Be attentive to what is taking place in the world and how events and crises impact the lives of your hearers.

My homiletics professor taught me to think about specific individuals when developing sermons. For example, in any given church, a seventy-three-year-old woman in the front row might be grieving because she just lost her husband. A thirty-five-year-old veteran toward the back of the auditorium may also be grieving because his wife left him for another man. A teen in the third row might be angry because his parents just separated. An inmate in a prison chapel may be fighting guilt because he isn't there for his children.

These are the real things happening in the real world to real people. Read your congregation and know what they are going through.

An Unlimited Supply of Sermon Ideas

After I began to read the Bible to be transformed by it rather than to merely find and develop sermons from it, I had more sermon ideas than I could shake a concordance at! Eventually, my preaching transitioned from being mildly interesting (on a good day), to being transformational. My motivation to preach was no longer derived from expectation as a senior pastor; I began to preach from a heart that was being transformed by the Holy Spirit through God's Word. I couldn't wait to share with others what God was teaching me and how He was changing me. I wanted every one of my church members to be transformed by God's Word, too.

Preaching-Effectiveness Continuum

When I exchanged my Rick-Warren-help-me attitude for a Holy-Spirit-change-me attitude, my sermons morphed from being interesting to impacting. I think of preaching effectiveness on a continuum. On one end are sermons that make us sleepy. On the other end are sermons that transform our lives:

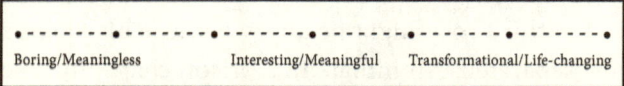

Many factors contribute to whether a sermon is boring, interesting, or transformational, including the preacher's skill level, preparation time, and spirituality. Unfortunately, too many sermons fall somewhere in the range of boring/meaningless to interesting/meaningful.

The problem is not necessarily a pastor's inability to write good sermons or his lack of homiletic giftedness. The problem may be that many pastors read the Bible with the wrong "motives." They read while seeking sermon-related information rather than heart-related transformation. If God's Word is going to transform others, it must first transform you.

Becoming a Transformer

In his sermon at Pentecost, Peter spoke passionately about the power of the Holy Spirit to accomplish His work in people's lives. Peter, who two months earlier had selfishly denied Christ three times, preached from a heart that had been transformed by Christ.

The Bible says that when the people heard Peter's sermon, *They were cut to the heart* (Acts 2:37). They were deeply moved and eager to respond to Peter's message. They said to him and the other apostles, *Brothers, what shall we do?*

Our words should cut to the heart, not bore to tears. Our listeners should be eager to respond, not eager to hear the words, "In closing."

Every time you preach, you have a God-ordained opportunity to be a transformer. But transformational preaching takes place only when we preachers allow God's transforming presence to cut our hearts first.

Chapter 8

Invite Hearers to Make
a Decision for Christ

When I (J.A.J.) met the beautiful young lady who would become my wife, I was quite nervous about asking for her phone number. I wanted to call her and ask her out, but what if she had no interest in going out with me? After all, I don't exactly look like Ryan Reynolds.

This lovely blue-eyed girl not only gave me her number, but she said "yes" when I invited her to go on a date with me. I was elated. She was way out of my league, but she said yes.

I look back at our first encounter with a smile. It's troubling to think about all I might have missed in life if I had chickened out and had not asked her out. We never would have married each other. We never would have shared our lives together. And we never would have had four incredible children together.

It all began with an invitation.

We believe that invitations are also crucial when communicating God's Word. Every time there are unbelievers in your audience and you do not give them an invitation to accept Jesus as their Lord and Savior, they miss an opportunity to begin a new life in Christ.

Ask for a Response

Every sermon you preach should conclude with a call to action. Your talk should take the hearers somewhere and invite them to do something: put more faith in God, change an attitude, gain a new perspective, give up a bad habit, share their faith with unbelievers, etc. However, it is also vital that you invite your hearers to make a decision to follow Christ. It may be that there are some in your audience who want to hand their lives over to Jesus but have no idea how to proceed. It would be a tragedy to send them home in such a state.

If you are preaching to a group of strong believers, a call to make a decision for Christ is most likely unnecessary. But if you suspect that there are unbelievers in your audience, end your talk by inviting people to pray the so-called "Sinner's Prayer."

Steps for Giving an Invitation

Step 1: Make a Transition Statement
Segue to the invitation by saying something like, "I believe God is speaking to many of our hearts today. I'm going to give an opportunity for you to respond to God's call with a prayer. Let's all bow our heads."

Step 2: Read the Sinner's Prayer

Before you ask your hearers to repeat the prayer after you, read it to them so they know what they are about to pray.

Note: The Sinner's Prayer follows a basic pattern with three components: sorry, please, and thank you.[15]

Sorry: Give people an invitation to confess sin.

Please: Give them an opportunity to ask God to save them.

Thank you: Thank God for His salvation through His Son, Jesus.

The theme of your Sinner's Prayer will be linked to the theme of your sermon. In other words, you won't just randomly give a Sinner's Prayer without it being tied in some way to your sermon; that would be confusing to your listeners.

For example, if your message focused on the story of Zacchaeus, here's what the Sinner's Prayer might look like in this sermon:

Luke 19:1-10: "O God, I am sorry that I have not lived the way You want me to live. Please come into my life, just like You did for Zacchaeus. Thank You for sending Jesus to seek and save the lost. Thank You for saving me."

For "Content in Christ," the expository sermon developed in chapter 1, here is how you can use the "sorry, please, thank you" pattern:

---

15 In *Evangelism in a Skeptical World* (p. 235), Sam Chan develops the "sorry, please, and thank you" formula. Here are a few of his examples:
Romans 3:21-31: "O God, sorry for falling short of Your glory. Please declare me innocent. Thank You that Jesus died for my sins."
John 3:16: "O God, sorry that I have not believed in Jesus. Please give me eternal life. Thank You for sending Jesus to save me."

Philippians 4:10-20: "O God, I am sorry that I have depended on my own strength and not on Yours. Please come into my life; I trust in Jesus to be my Savior. Thank You for sending Jesus to the cross to die for my sins and for saving me."

That is how you develop a Sinner's Prayer. In summary, in Step 2 you will read the prayer to your audience so they know exactly what they will be asking God to do.

Step 3: Invite People to Pray the Sinner's Prayer

After you read the prayer, say something like, "If this sounds like something you want to say to God, then I invite you to pray this prayer with me. I will pray it one sentence at a time, and then I am going to pause so that you can say that same sentence in your heart to God."

Then pray the Sinner's Prayer one sentence at a time. Be sure to give a long pause between each sentence. You can also invite your hearers to repeat the prayer phrase by phrase rather than sentence by sentence.

Step 4: Explain What Just Happened

After you've led someone in the Sinner's Prayer, say something like, "If you prayed that prayer and have sincerely believed in Jesus Christ for the forgiveness of your sin, the Bible says that you are saved! You might feel different, or maybe you don't. But God has heard you, and He is rejoicing! Today you have begun a new life in Christ."

This is a true time to celebrate, so maybe ask the group to clap and cheer. It's exciting when someone surrenders his/her life to Christ. I'm always amazed by how the reciting of the Sinner's Prayer is so often followed by what seems to be total indifference. How sad! It should be celebrated for the joyful event it is.

Step 5: Follow Up

It is not enough just to lead others into a prayer of salvation. When someone receives Christ as his or her Savior, the person then needs help to begin the process of discipleship.

You need to decide how you will follow up with those who have accepted Christ. One option is to say something like, "For those of you who just received Christ as your Lord and Savior, I'd love to meet you. I'm inviting you to come meet me after we dismiss." (Be sure to give a location where they can meet you.)

Then explain why you want to meet with them: "Talking to me, a stranger, might be kind of scary. I know I look intimidating [smile]. But the reason I'm asking you to do this is so I can connect you with other Christians who can help you grow in your faith."

I once planted a church that met in a junior high school gym. We set up several tables (like booths at a convention) near the entrance to the gym. One table was hosted by a team that made free espresso and coffee drinks for those in attendance. At another table, people could sign up to be a part of various ministries, such as the dance ministry or the softball ministry. But we also had a "Yes!" table, which was how we followed up with those who made a decision for Christ.

I asked those who responded to the invitation at the conclusion of the sermon to visit the "Yes!" table after the service was dismissed. Several church members hosted this table. They gave new believers a Bible study and a "Yes!" booklet that walked these new converts through the basic fundamentals of the faith. The "Yes!" team members asked every person who visited the table if they would like to meet with them for coffee during the week to discuss the contents of the "Yes!" booklet. The "Yes!" ministry was the primary way we helped new believers begin their new journey with Christ.

It is vital to think of a method of follow-up. Depending on the layout of your meeting place, you may need to be creative. But without follow-up, your hearers will not know how to take their first few steps in their new walk with Christ. The enemy will do all he can to divert people from the decision they made to follow Christ.

When you write your sermons, outline how you will invite people to receive Christ as their Savior. Write a Sinner's Prayer that ties into the theme of your message, and be prepared to give an invitation at the conclusion of your sermon.

My wife was sure happy that I invited her to go out with me. Both of our lives changed because of it, and we produced four amazing children. You will bring much joy to those whom you invite to accept Christ, for their lives may be forever changed because of it.

Chapter 9

Preach Under
Divine Influence

This book contains plenty of tools and techniques to help you build life-transformational sermons. We've presented several best practices of sermon writing, showing you effective ways to create expository, topical, Bible-story, and interactive sermons.

The best preaching methods, however, are meaningless if the sermon itself isn't soaked in prayer. We must be in constant communion with God when we prepare and write our sermons, and when we present them. If not, our preparation time, in the words of John Piper, is nothing but a time of "insipid academic gamesmanship."

Think about Piper's statement for a moment. We may have good exegesis and be able to explain how a text applies to modern readers, but we're merely playing lifeless intellectual games if we are not communing with God and inviting Christ's Spirit to illuminate our thoughts and ideas. "Fruitful study and fervent prayer live and die together. . . . Without the spirit of constant prayer, we cannot maintain the gravity and gladness that lingers in the vicinity of the throne of grace."[16]

Without the power and preparation of prayer, our preaching becomes fleshly, not Spirit-filled. Paul wrote often about the dangers of giving opportunity to the flesh and allowing it to *gratify its desires* (Romans 13:14; Galatians 5:16).

Peter also warned believers of *the passions of the flesh, which wage war against your soul* (1 Peter 2:11). You may desire to do God's will and preach God's Word from a godly motive, but these things can easily be ruined by ungodly means.

Watchman Nee wrote of the fleshly preacher:

> To them, working for the Lord is of supreme importance, but often they forget the Lord who gives work. The Lord's work becomes the center, the Lord of work recedes to the background. . . . They may depend on God, but they likewise depend on self. They expend more time in analyzing, in collecting materials, and in hard thinking than in prayer, on seeking God's mind, and on waiting for the power from above. . . . With such an approach as this, these believers will naturally put more confidence in the message than in the Lord.[17]

---

16   John Piper, *The Supremacy of God in Preaching* (Grand Rapids: Baker Books, 2015), 65-66.

17   Watchman Nee, *The Spiritual Man*, vol. 1 (New York: Christian Fellowship Publishers, 1977), 160-162.

Preparatory prayer exposes our motives to God and allows His Spirit to examine and exhort our hearts.

The Lord Jesus is our prime example of a man who prayed. Before preaching a word in His public ministry, He initiated that anointing with prayer at His baptism (Luke 3:21-22). Despite His travels, He rose *very early in the morning, while it was still dark* (Mark 1:35), and separated Himself from all distractions in order to be in prayer. He knew that He must pray before preaching; such was the pattern of His life. He demonstrated that communion with God was not just essential to His calling, but was the identity of His character.

We might think that since He is the Son of God, there would be no need for Him to pray. How could He ever need direction or guidance for His life circumstances or His earthly ministry? What could He not know for which He would need to seek God's will or instruction? Jesus did not pray because of uncertainty, insufficiency, or doubt. He did not pray for divine help to cover for His human flaws (for there were none). Rather, He prayed because it was the nature of His life and His relationship with His father. He prayed because as man, He learned how to obey and depend on God while passing through the experience of human suffering (Hebrews 5:8). He prayed because He could find refreshment for His weary soul in communication with His Father, and could enjoy fellowship with the only one who truly knew Him (Psalm 16:2; 23:3; 54:4; 63:5-8). He prayed because He was the perfect servant and Son. *He would withdraw to desolate places and pray* (Luke 5:16). His prayer life anointed His practice in life.

Every preacher must be faithful to pray. We must

trust the Lord and pour out our hearts before Him in order to receive from Him (Psalm 62:8). The Puritan preacher Cotton Mather is an example of one who carefully intertwined study and prayer. He stopped at the end of every paragraph as he wrote his sermon "to pray and examine himself and try to fix on his heart some holy impression of his subject."[18]

This type of devotion to both the Word and prayer will produce sermons that are shaped by the convicting power of the Holy Spirit. The person who preaches must be a person who prays. This is nonnegotiable. Following are five reasons why.

Prayer keeps you dependent on the Holy Spirit.

Your preparation time is also your prayer time, in which you are seeking the Lord's help. Be especially reliant on the Holy Spirit for discernment in interpreting Scripture since the Holy Spirit makes us receptive to the Bible. The Holy Spirit assists us through the interpretive journey in several ways:

- He gives us the discipline to study well.

- He gives us the humility to accept the truth we find without twisting it.

- He is faithful to give us a desperately needed discovery or insight in His providential guidance of our work.[19]

---

18 Piper, *Supremacy*, 66.
19 Piper, *Supremacy*, 47-48.

A proper understanding of the Word of God requires words with God. Since the Spirit is the author of Scripture, why not ask Him what it means and how it should impact our lives?

While reading the words of Jeremiah the prophet, Daniel turned his face to the Lord and prayed, accompanied with fasting and confession. After a lengthy time of intimate prayer, God answered, and Gabriel gave Daniel insight and understanding about what he had read. In fact, God revealed even more fully to Daniel the prophetic truths of the Messiah's coming at the end of days (Daniel 9:2-4, 20-22).

When faced with opposition to the preaching of the Word, the early church recognized that their strength would only come from above (Psalm 121:1-2). They sought help from the Spirit who had called them to be witnesses, and *they lifted their voices together to God* (Acts 4:24), praying for boldness to continue preaching the truth. No ministry will reap success if prayer is not sown from the start. We must depend on the Lord.

Yield to the Holy Spirit as you prepare your sermons. You can expect God to give you insightful observations when you do so. Ask Him for wisdom, guidance, direction and insight. Let the Holy Spirit lead you. A. W. Tozer rightly said, "If we are to be the voice of God in our generation, we must be illuminated by the Holy Spirit."[20]

Ask God for help. Listen. Rely on His Spirit. Your listeners' spiritual welfare depends on it.

---

20   A. W. Tozer, *Voice of a Prophet* (Minneapolis: Bethany House, 2014), 119.

Prayer makes you a Spirit-empowered preacher.

We must depend on the Holy Spirit not only for help, but also for power. Without the Spirit's presence and power, our sermons and their delivery will be lifeless and dry, like salt lacking flavor – *no longer good for anything* (Matthew 5:13).

The apostle Paul told the Corinthian believers that his speech and his message *were not in plausible words of wisdom, but in demonstration of the Spirit and of power, so that [their] faith might not rest in the wisdom of men but in the power of God* (1 Corinthians 2:4-5). Paul preached under the divine influence of the Spirit; every word he uttered was inspired by the Spirit and delivered in God's power.

It is crucial that we draw from and demonstrate this divine power. Without it, nothing of any lasting value will be achieved no matter how many people may admire our persuasive words, enjoy our illustrations, or learn from our doctrine. This is because the Spirit empowers not only the speaker to speak, but also the hearer to hear. Our prayers should be both for our hearts and for those of our listeners to receive the Word of God (Colossians 4:3).

To be Spirit-empowered preachers, we allow God to break us of our self-reliance and self-assurance. Paul preached *in weakness and in fear and much trembling* (1 Corinthians 2:3). I (J.A.J.) once asked my dad if he still got nervous when he preached. He was a lifelong preacher who spoke to various audiences as a missionary and a pastor. He said, "Yes, I still get nervous; and I hope it never stops. As soon as your knees stop knocking, you've lost your effectiveness."

My dad was referring to the danger of self-reliance. He was aware that he needed God for strength and power. In humility, we must admit that without God we can do nothing of any eternal value (John 15:5). God's power will be released in us only when we acknowledge our dependence on Him.

Prayer helps you be attentive to God's voice.

Our lives are cluttered with much commotion. Our schedules are crammed with much to do and little time to do it. We're busy. We're stressed. We live in a whirlwind of activity and noise.

When we study for our sermons, if we're not careful, we can hastily approach God's Word and blink at our responsibility to pray. Failure to quiet our hearts and listen for God's voice can easily and unintentionally sideline all that God wants to speak to us. God will still work despite our flagrant failures, but we miss out on blessing when we're irresponsible stewards of His ministry.

The activity of praying is easy, although the discipline to do so is not. Prayer requires patience. In Jeremiah's afflictions, he maintained a posture of prayer and expectations: *It is good that one should wait quietly for the salvation of the* LORD (Lamentations 3:26). He understood that the Lord wants His people to call on Him so that He can reveal the *great and hidden things* that they *have not known* (Jeremiah 33:3).

When David was anxious because evildoers were prospering, he told his heart, *Be still before the LORD and wait patiently for him* (Psalm 37:7). When God told the Israelites that He would be exalted among all nations, He said, *Be still, and know that I am God* (Psalm 46:10). Even Jesus *dismissed the crowds* and *went up on the mountain by himself to pray . . . alone* (Matthew 14:23).

If we are to experience God and hear His voice, we must choke out all of the clamor in our lives and still ourselves. It is in that stillness that God will speak to your heart, and it is in that stillness that He will give us a timely word that breathes life into our congregations. A. W. Tozer said, "Those [persons] who were mightily used of God, who became a voice of God in their generation, heard that voice in the quiet and stillness of their own hearts."[21]

Prayer makes you a heart-healthy preacher

The change we long to see in our listener's hearts must first be in ourselves, but that will not happen until we probe the inner workings of our hearts through prayer. The "great lack" of many preachers, according to E. M. Bounds, is not a lack of sermon preparation, but a "lack of holiness. . . . We do not meditate on God and his Word and watch and fast and pray enough. The heart is the great hindrance to our preaching."[22]

When you prepare your sermons, take David's

---

21 Tozer, *Voice*, 118.
22 E. M. Bounds, *Power Through Prayer* (Chicago: Moody Publishing, 2009), 76-77.

prayer of examination into your study time: *Search me, O God, and know my heart! Try me and know my thoughts! And see if there be any grievous way in me, and lead me in the way everlasting!* (Psalm 139:23-24). As you read a verse or passage of Scripture, check your heart against the message of the text. Pause to ask God to examine your heart. Is there a habitual sin you need to surrender? Is there an attitude you must change? Is there a command you need to obey? Is there an example you should follow?

When you invite God to search your heart, He will show you areas in your life that need to be surrendered to Him, such as pride, selfish ambition, covetousness, jealousy, lust, a hot temper, and resentment – to name just a few of the heart problems we are prone to. Then, as God shows you any grievous way, confess it and repent. Such a process purifies your heart, which in turn prepares your heart to preach. Bounds notes, "A prepared heart is much better than a prepared sermon. A prepared heart will make a prepared sermon."[23]

How could Ezra have been as effective in his ministry without prayer? Before preaching to the people, he prayed with them, joining them in humble confession. Then the Lord convicted their hearts and moved them to act (Ezra 9:1-12). We can't expect the message to impact our listeners unless we first let the Word try our own hearts.

Prayer makes a way for us to preach with clean hearts, freeing us to preach with authenticity. With a heart that has been examined on God's operating table,

---

23   Bounds, *Power*, 76.

we can call our listeners to experience what we have experienced ourselves. The passion to preach without the discipline to pray is just a desire to perform. Be a heart-healthy preacher – one who continually invites God to shape your heart.

Prayer cultivates your devotion to God.

Just like a devoted husband desires to spend time with his wife, so a devoted preacher desires to spend time with his Savior. Martha was busy for the Lord, but was *anxious and troubled about many things*. Mary had *chosen the good portion* (Luke 10:39-42). She is often mentioned as being at the feet of the Lord (e.g., John 11:32; 12:3).

We have an even greater privilege than Mary, who sat at His feet on earth; we are able to *draw near with a true heart in full assurance of faith* (Hebrews 10:22) and are seated *with him in the heavenly places in Christ Jesus* (Ephesians 2:6). Although we are physically on earth, we are spiritually with Him in the heavenly sanctuary when we pray. This is access that no Old Testament saint ever enjoyed. And as with husband and wife, a relationship is based on regular communion and communication. We must desire Him.

Moses said to the Lord, *Please show me your glory* (Exodus 33:18). David wrote, *O Lord, I love the habitation of your house and the place where your glory dwells* (Psalm 26:8). His true desire was to *dwell in the house of the Lord* and *gaze upon the beauty of the Lord* (Psalm 27:4).

It is no coincidence that these men were used so

mightily by the Lord, for they knew Him in such an intimate way.

Growing closer to the Lord and spending time with Him should ignite a desire in us to grow closer to Him still. As God gives more, it stimulates a desire to know more, the limits of which we will never reach for all eternity.

Prayer is one of the greatest signs of our devotion to God. When we are submitted to His lordship, we gladly accept the call to *pray without ceasing* (1 Thessalonians 5:17), for we long to fellowship with Him.

If you choose to spend your life communicating God's Word to others, you must receive clear communication from God. Half-hearted devotion to Him will not cut it. Our listeners need preachers who are all in, who make Christ their greatest treasure. It is not enough for us to be exegetically sound and know how to develop well-crafted sermons. While these things are important and valuable, what is needed are preachers who are in constant communion with God, inspired by His Spirit, and surrendered to Him in complete devotion. That's the kind of preacher God can use – really use.

Before we can effectively exercise our call to preach, we must submit to the command to pray. We will only be a conduit of divine power if we commune with and are confident in the person who is the source of all power. Even the disciples, having been with Jesus, saw in Him the pattern of divine service and Spirit-filled living. They said, *Lord, teach us to pray* (Luke 11:1).

It is not great talents or great learning or great

preachers that God needs, but men great in holiness, great in faith, great in love, great in fidelity, and great for God – men who are always preaching by holy sermons in the pulpit and by holy lives out of it. These can mold a generation for God.[24]

Be such a preacher.

---

24 Bounds, *Power*, 21.

Final Word

This gospel of the kingdom will be proclaimed throughout the whole world as a testimony to all nations. —Matthew 24:14

Then I saw another angel flying directly overhead, with an eternal gospel to proclaim to those who dwell on earth, to every nation and tribe and language and people. —Revelation 14:6

We have presented various types of sermons in this book to help you prepare sermons that will hopefully keep your hearers on the edges of their seats while inspiring them to take action.

You will no doubt write various types of sermons with various subjects, but they should all have the same theme: the gospel. Regardless of the kind of sermon you preach, always keep Christ's redemptive work at the forefront.

The primary goal of every preacher is to direct people

to Christ. All Scripture speaks of Him and of God's plan to redeem humankind through Him (Luke 24:27; John 5:39). Therefore, every preacher must be familiar with and grounded in the gospel: *that Christ died for our sins in accordance with the Scriptures, that he was buried, that he was raised on the third day in accordance with the Scriptures* (1 Corinthians 15:3-4).

Whether preaching to Jew or gentile, the apostle Paul centered his message on Jesus Christ. When confronting Jews, he preached forgiveness and justification through the one who fulfilled the Law and freed humankind (Acts 13:38-39). When reasoning with gentiles, he revealed the *Lord of heaven* (Acts 17:24) who *commands all people everywhere to repent, because he has fixed a day which he will judge the world in righteousness by a man whom he has appointed; and of this he has given assurance to all by raising him from the dead* (Acts 17:30-31). Paul testified faithfully *both to Jews and to the Greeks of repentance toward God and of faith in our Lord Jesus Christ* (Acts 20:21).

Since the fall of man, God has continually provided the means by which the gospel could reach humanity. The prophets and writers of Old Testament Scripture pieced together progressive revelation that came *at many times and in many ways* (Hebrews 1:1). Today we have the truth fully revealed in Christ through His past, present, and future work.

The everlasting, ageless, timeless, and marvelous gospel has never lost its relevance or effectiveness and will be made available for humankind right to the end of time. It is *the power of God for salvation to everyone who believes* (Romans 1:16).

The gospel will also be the joy of every believer even on into eternity. When the servants of God worship Him forever in a new heaven and new earth, what theme will be carried out in that worship? *Worthy is the lamb who was slain, to receive power and wealth and wisdom and might and honor and glory and blessing . . . forever and ever!* (Revelation 5:12-13; see also Revelation 22:3). God never loses sight or appreciation of Christ, and neither should we.

Keep the gospel at the forefront of any Scripture text or sermon content because glorifying Christ brings glory to God. As we preach to the audiences to which God has assigned us, may we be able to say along with the apostle Paul, *Woe to me if I do not preach the gospel!* (1 Corinthians 9:16).

Prepping for a Sermon or Bible Study

It is vital to invest time preparing for your sermon or Bible study, but don't read and study just for knowledge. As you study, let God's Word penetrate your heart and draw you closer to Him. Your goal is not just to develop a good sermon or Bible study, but to allow the transforming power of God's Spirit to change you. Before you proclaim biblical truth to others, you should live out that truth yourself, or at least be convicted to do so. Your number one goal should be spiritual transformation, not the transfer of information. Following are some steps to help you.

Step 1: Pray

Pray before and during your prep time, and rely on the Holy Spirit to illuminate God's Word. This is the most important step.

Step 2: Select Your Text

A "text" can be any portion of Scripture, from part of a verse to an entire passage. Such passages are easy to detect if you use a study Bible, which typically divides Scripture into sections that are denoted by headings. In the ESV Study Bible, for example, Philippians 4:10-20 is titled "God's Provision." This section is a passage of Scripture that centers on a theme/thought. When deciding on a text for study, choose from an area of Scripture that you have been reading or has spoken to you, that you understand and appreciate, and that has context and meaning that fits the theme of your message.

Step 3: Gather Available Resources

Many study materials have been created to help believers look deeply into Scripture. Study Bibles, concordances, Bible dictionaries, commentaries, Bible handbooks, etc. are all helpful tools when preparing for a Bible study or sermon.

Step 4: Embark on the Interpretive Journey

Now you're ready to roll up your sleeves and get to work. In this step, you will exegete your selected passage. This means that you will uncover the intended meaning of the text and discover the theological principles or biblical truths contained in that text. You will then help your listeners embrace the message so that the Spirit might conform their lives to these theological principles or biblical truths (which we will refer to from this point on as Bible truths).

You will address five questions:

Question 1: What did the text mean to the original audience?

Question 2: What are the differences between the original audience and us?

Question 3: What are the Bible truths in the text?

Question 4: How do the Bible truths fit with the rest of Scripture?

Question 5: How should Christians today live out the Bible truths through faith in Christ?

When these questions are answered, you'll have a sound grasp on the passage of your study. Let's look at each of these questions.

Question 1: What did the text mean to the original **audience?**

Examine the historical, cultural, and literary context in this step. This is where commentaries, study Bibles, handbooks, etc. can be helpful.

You should be able to answer the following questions:

- Who wrote the book that contains your passage?

- Why was it written?

- What were the circumstances?

- What type of writing is it (poetry, narrative, epistle, apocalyptic, etc.) and why is knowing this important? The literary context will help you determine how to approach the text. For example, if you're reading the Psalms, pay attention to such things as metaphors, similes, and figures of speech (e.g., *My tears have been my food day and night* – Psalm 42:3).

- What relationship did the author have with his readers?

- Who was the original audience?

- What was their relationship to God?

- What was the nature of the author's relationship with God?

Read the passage carefully several times. Also read the chapter that precedes the passage and the chapter that follows it. This will help you get a bigger picture of what's going on in your selected passage.

Once you have a good overall grasp of your passage in context, write a one or two sentence summary of it. This is to make sure that you clearly understand what's going on in the passage.

Question 2: What are the differences between the original audience and **us?**

Next, make a list of ways in which the situation of the passage is different from our situation today. Here are a few things to consider:

- Is it under an Old Testament covenant?

- Does it involve a king?

- Is it written to the Jewish people?

- Does it concern a specific command from God (e.g., "Noah, build an ark.")?

It is important to know such things because there is a change in situations between the Old and New Testaments, and there is a huge span of time between them and us. The differences do not mean that the Bible truth doesn't apply to us; it simply means that we must take the differences into consideration when we determine the meaning of the text.

Question 3: What are the Bible truths in the **text?**

Determine what God wants us to learn from the passage. In question 2, you discovered the differences between the original audience and us. Now you will identify Bible truths that are true despite the differences across time periods and cultures. If you look for a Bible truth within a passage that applies to a specific occasion or people (e.g., the law against eating pork, which is found in Leviticus 11), you must identify the principle that applies equally to both then and now, even if the specific, literal details do not. For example, in the Old Testament, Jews practiced ceremonial holiness. Today we rely on Jesus for our holiness, making the old-covenant food practices obsolete. The Bible truth in Leviticus 11 that applies to them and us is that God is holy and wants us to be holy.

Write down the Bible truths found in your passage, and then ask and answer:

- Is the Bible truth reflected in the text?

- Is it timeless and not tied to a specific situation?

- Is it culturally bound?

- Does it correspond with the teaching of the rest of Scripture?

- Is it relevant to both the original and contemporary readers? How?

If you answered no to any of these questions, refine the Bible truth you extracted. If you are preparing for a sermon, this is the step that will help you develop your Big Idea. The Big Idea is the single, all-encompassing concept of your sermon – the one major idea. The points of your sermon will be built around this one grand thought.

Final note for question 3: When you discover a Bible truth in Scripture, it is important to emphasize that Jesus is the ultimate fulfillment of that Scripture. Whatever obstacle or problem we face, Jesus faced it and did so without sinning. No matter what passage you use for your Bible study or sermon, point your listeners to Jesus, assuring them that only through faith in Him can they successfully live out the Bible truth. For example, we cannot be holy through what we eat or do not eat. We can only be holy by abiding in Christ.

Question 4: How do the Bible truths fit with the rest of **Scripture?**

If your Bible truth is in conflict with other parts of Scripture, it is invalid. Go back to question 3.

Question 5: How should Christians today live out the Bible truths through faith in **Christ?**

This step is called application. Come up with real-life situations in which the Bible truth might apply. Think of your audience and their needs. Are there some people in your Bible study or listeners in your audience who are estranged from their children? Are some people hurting because their spouses walked away from them? Are individuals struggling with addictions? These are real-life issues.

Step 5: Review

Go back over the notes you took on the Interpretive Journey. Fill in any gaps or holes you find. Look for any unanswered questions and seek to answer them. Try to anticipate points of potential confusion for your hearers, and provide clarification. Make all appropriate revisions. Once you've completed all of the above steps, you are ready to begin writing your sermon or creating a Bible study.

Sample Big Ideas and Sermon Outlines

Here are some examples of Big Ideas and corresponding sermon points that develop these Big Ideas:

Text: Luke 12:13-21

Big Idea: A fool worships the gift, but a wise person worships God, the giver.

Points: Why does God call the rich man a fool?

- God calls the rich man a fool because he lives for himself.

- God calls the rich man a fool because he stores up what cannot last.

- God calls the rich man a fool because he lives as if he will never die.

You could also make an action-oriented presentation of these points:

Points: If you are to be rich toward God, there are three things you cannot do:

- You cannot live for yourself.

- You cannot store up what cannot last.

- You cannot live as if you will never die.

Here is another way you could present these points:

- Don't live for yourself.

- Don't store up what cannot last.

- Don't live as if you will never die.

Text: John 3:16

Big Idea: God shows His love by sending His Son, Jesus.

Points: How do I know God loves me?

- I know God loves me because He sent His Son.

- I know God loves me because all I have to do is believe in His Son to be rescued from perishing.

- I know God loves me because God will give me eternal life.

Text: 2 Timothy 4:1-5

Big Idea: Because God will judge sin, we must proclaim His Word for the purposes He intends.

Points: Because God will judge sin:

- We must proclaim His Word to rescue the needy.

- We must proclaim His Word to defend the truth.

- We must proclaim His Word to fulfill our duty.

Resource 3

A Quick Guide for Preaching a Three-Point Sermon

The most important thing to remember when you preach a sermon is that you have two responsibilities: the truth of the Bible and the spiritual needs of the listeners.

There are many, many ways to develop and deliver a sermon. If you don't have much experience developing an expository sermon, the following will guide you through the process of creating a three-point sermon based upon a passage of Scripture.

Step 1: Sermon Introduction

In this step you will get your listeners ready for the sermon by creating interest in your topic and immediately grabbing their attention. You want everyone on the same page. There are many ways to do this. Some are listed below:

- Tell a story that relates to the theme of your sermon.

- Share/play a piece of music that connects to your sermon.

- Recount a movie scene or television show that correlates to your sermon.

- Spotlight a common need that your sermon addresses.

Be creative.

Note: Although the introduction happens first in your sermon, it is much easier to develop it after you have written your whole sermon.

Step 2: State the Big Idea

Your introduction must take you to your Big Idea. The Big Idea is the central idea or main focus of your sermon. It is a statement from which your whole message emerges. Your three points will be built around this one grand thought. Here is an example of a Big Idea for a sermon on Psalm 15: "God has made a way for us to stand firm forever."

Step 3: Pray

Ask God to illuminate the text and to reveal His message in His Word (or use words to that effect). Make your prayer your own.

Step 4: Read the Bible Passage

(Or ask a volunteer to read the text aloud.)

Step 5: Restate the Big Idea and Reveal Point 1

If your Big Idea is "God has made a way for us to stand firm forever," your first point might be "God wants us to walk blamelessly and do what is right" (Psalm 15:2). In your sermon, you would restate your Big Idea at this time and then say something like, "If we are going to stand firm forever, there are three things we must do. The first thing we must do is walk blamelessly and do what is right."

Use the acronym EAR to help you develop your points:

Explain It (E): Now you will explain the text itself, highlighting the section that reveals Point 1. You might need to elaborate using historical, cultural, or literary context (work you did in Question 1 of the Interpretive Journey in your prep work). Also, you may note other Bible passages that further clarify the section. Always let Scripture interpret Scripture.

Anticipate Objections (A): In this part, you address any potential questions or objections that your listeners may be thinking. For example, if your point is "Don't be distracted by your abundance," some of your listeners may be thinking, "How can I be distracted by my abundance? Things are finally working out for me!" Your explanation must answer those questions. You might introduce an objection by saying, "You may be thinking that . . ." or "How can it be that . . .?"

Relate It (R): Relate your point and explanation through illustrations and application. Use creative ways (quote, song, story, etc.) that can help your listeners connect the text to their lives with simple understanding. Then give an application for the point you are highlighting. During your prep time, you came up with real-life situations addressed by the Bible truths in your passage. This is now the point in your sermon where you will explain how these truths apply to everyday Christian living.

Steps 6 and 7: Develop Points 2 and 3

Develop Points 2 and 3 in the same way as with Point 1.

When delivering your sermon, you will need to make a transitional statement between your points. Here is an example of such a statement for our hypothetical Point 1. At the end of Point 1, you might say, "So if we are to stand together as God wants, we must walk blamelessly before Him and do what is right. The second thing we must do is . . ." Do you see how we restated the Big Idea and Point 1? This will reiterate the central theme of the sermon while indicating to your hearers that you are moving on to the next section.

Step 8: Closing

Close by making Jesus the hero. You'll address the question, "Now what?" What are your listeners to do now? You can give a call to action, but you must impress upon them that they *cannot* make any meaningful, lasting changes without faith in Jesus. Only He can change our hearts and enable us to be godly. He is our perfect model and our strength. The little we can do, we do *through Christ*, who strengthens us.

Step 9: Pray

Don't summarize or preach a sermon in your prayer. Instead, speak succinctly and intercede for your audience. Remember that *He* is gracious and able, and *we* are needy and weak. Don't lose the attention of your audience by wordiness, but don't treat the closing prayer as just a formality either. Ask God to continue to move in everyone's heart.

Final Note: Think through your transitions. How will you transition between E, A, and R, and between the points of your sermon?

Resource 4

Outline Your Sermon

1. Introduction/Anticipatory Set:
2. Big Idea:
3. Pray:
4. Read the Bible passage:
5. Point 1:
   - E (Explain.):
   - A (Anticipate objections.):
   - R (Relate your point through illustrations and application.):
6. Point 2:
   - E:
   - A:
   - R:
7. Point 3:
   - E:
   - A:
   - R:
8. Close by making Jesus the hero.
9. Pray.

Bible-Story Sermon Worksheet

Sermon Title:
Biblical Text:

Introduction
Prayer:
How will you set up the story?
How will you introduce the story's relevance?

First Half of the Sermon Body
Which verses need to be explained so hearers understand context? List and explain.

Second Half of the Sermon Body
What is your transitional statement?
What three observations will you make? (Develop each observation using the EAR method.)

1.

2.

3.

Closing

How will you apply the story? (What do you want your hearers to do?)

What response will you ask for?

Prayer:

Resource 6

One Hundred Bible Stories

This resource provides a list of one hundred stories that you can develop into Bible-story sermons. Several of the stories below have many stories within the overarching story. For example, there are several stories within the story of Joseph (Genesis 37-50) that can be preached as independent sermons.

The list below will point you to great stories. The titles describe the contents of the story, but you should give a creative title to your sermon that best captures the content of your message.

1. The story of creation and the fall (Genesis 1-2)

2. The fall of man (Genesis 3)

3. Noah and the flood (Genesis 6:9-9:17)

4. The tower of Babel (Genesis 11:1-9)

5. Three visitors to Abraham (Genesis 18:1-15)

6. The story of Joseph (Genesis 37-50)

7. The birth of Moses (Exodus 1:8-2:10)

8. Moses and the burning bush (Exodus 3:1-15)

9. The ten plagues (Exodus 7:6-11:10)

10. Crossing the Red Sea (Exodus 13:17-14:31)

11. Manna and the quail (Exodus 16)

12. Exploring Canaan (Numbers 13:1-14:12)

13. Balaam's donkey (Numbers 22:21-38)

14. The Ten Commandments (Deuteronomy 5:1-22)

15. The death of Moses (Deuteronomy 34)

16. Entering the Promised Land (Joshua 3)

17. The fall of Jericho (Joshua 5:13-6:27)

18. Deborah leads God's people (Judges 4-5)

19. Gideon fights the Midianites (Judges 6-7)

20. Samson and Delilah (Judges 16)

21. Ruth and Naomi (Ruth 1-4)

22. Israel asks for a king (1 Samuel 8)

23. God chooses David as king (1 Samuel 16:1-13)

24. David and Goliath (1 Samuel 17)

25. David becomes king (2 Samuel 5:1-12)

26. David and Bathsheba (2 Samuel 11)

27. Solomon's wisdom (1 Kings 3:16-28)

28. Solomon builds the temple (1 Kings 6)

29. Israel rebels against Rehoboam (1 Kings 12:1-24)

30. Elijah and the prophets of Baal (1 Kings 18:16-46)

31. The still small voice (1 Kings 19)

32. Elijah taken to heaven in a chariot (2 Kings 2:1-12)

33. Judah taken into exile (2 Kings 24-25)

34. The people return from exile (Ezra 1)

35. Isaiah's vision of God (Isaiah 6:1-8)

36. Isaiah's prophecies about the Messiah (Isaiah 7:10-17)

37. Isaiah's message of comfort (Isaiah 40:1-11)

38. The suffering servant (Isaiah 52:13-53:12)

39. Jeremiah and the potter's house (Jeremiah 18)

40. Jeremiah and the new covenant (Jeremiah 31:1-34)

41. Ezekiel's vision of a chariot (Ezekiel 1)

42. Ezekiel's vision of dry bones (Ezekiel 37:1-14)

43. The fiery furnace (Daniel 3)

44. Daniel and the lion's den (Daniel 6)

45. Hosea marries a promiscuous woman (Hosea 1)

46. Joel's vision of the future (Joel 2:28-32)

47. Amos condemns a king (Amos 7:10-17)

48. The story of Jonah (Jonah 1-4)

49. The promise of a Savior (Luke 1:26-38)

50. The birth of Jesus (Luke 2:1-7)

51. The shepherds and angels (Luke 2:8-20)

52. The wise men visit Jesus (Matthew 2:1-12)

53. Jesus is taken to the temple (Luke 2:22-40)

54. The escape to Egypt (Matthew 2:13-23)

55. Jesus gets lost in the temple (Luke 2:41-52)

56. John the Baptist announces Jesus (Matthew 3:1-12)

57. John is baptized (Mark 1:9-11)

58. Jesus is tempted in the wilderness (Luke 4:1-13)

59. Jesus calls the first disciples (Mark 1:16-20)

60. Jesus turns water into wine (John 2:1-11)

61. Jesus heals a paralyzed man (Mark 2:1-12)

62. Jesus talks to a Samaritan woman (John 4:4-42)

63. Jesus calms a storm (Matthew 8:23-27)

64. Jesus heals Jairus's daughter (Mark 5:21-43)

65. John the Baptist is beheaded (Matthew 14:1-12)

66. Jesus feeds the five thousand (John 6:1-15)

67. Jesus walks on water (Matthew 14:22-33)

68. Peter recognizes Jesus as the Messiah (Mark 8:27-30)

69. The transfiguration of Jesus (Luke 9:28-36)

70. The woman caught in adultery (John 8:1-11)

71. Jesus heals a man born blind (John 9)

72. The good Samaritan (Luke 10:25-37)

73. Mary, Martha, and Jesus (Luke 10:38-42)

74. The resurrection of Lazarus (John 11:1-44)

75. The prodigal son (Luke 15:11-32)

76. The rich man and Lazarus (Luke 16:19-31)

77. The story of Zacchaeus (Luke 19:1-10)

78. Mary anoints Jesus's feet (John 12:1-8)

79. Jesus washes the disciples' feet (John 13:1-30)

80. The Last Supper (Mark 14:12-26)

81. Jesus is arrested (John 18:1-13)

82. Peter denies Jesus (Luke 22:54-62)

83. The death of our Savior (Mark 15:20-41)

84. Jesus is buried (Matthew 27:57-66)

85. The resurrection of Jesus (Matthew 28:1-15)

86. The road to Emmaus (Luke 24:13-35)

87. Mary meets the risen Lord (John 20:1-18)

88. The Great Commission (Matthew 28:16-20)

89. Jesus restores Peter (John 21)

90. Jesus ascends into heaven (Acts 1:4-11)

91. The Holy Spirit descends on the disciples (Acts 2:1-13)

92. The story of Ananias and Sapphira (Acts 5:1-11)

93. The stoning of Stephen (Acts 6:8-7:1, 7:54-60)

94. The conversion of Saul (Acts 9:1-19)

95. Peter in prison (Acts 12:1-17)

96. The council in Jerusalem (Acts 15)

97. Paul and Silas in prison (Acts 16:16-40)

98. Paul preaches in Athens (Acts 17:16-34)

99. Paul is shipwrecked (Acts 27:1-28:15)

100. Paul preaches in Rome (Acts 28:16-31)

Preaching to the Least of These

This appendix is geared specifically for those who preach to and minister among *the least of these* (Matthew 25:40), including inmates in prison and individuals in homeless shelters, women's shelters, and recovery centers. It also applies to incarcerated believers who find themselves called to share the gospel and preach sermons to their fellow inmates. These are precious audiences often overlooked by society and even by the broader church, yet they are dear to the heart of Jesus, who said, *I was in prison and you came to me* (Matthew 25:36).

Sermons That Cut to the Heart Must Be Gospel-Centered

For any sermon to truly pierce the heart, it must proclaim the gospel of Jesus Christ. Jesus is the answer to every problem faced by humanity, and especially those of the marginalized and broken. The gospel is the power of God for salvation (Romans 1:16), and it brings healing to the deepest wounds of the soul.

Preaching to the least of these requires a deep sensitivity to the burdens they carry. It also demands a clear and unwavering focus on the gospel – not shallow advice or moralism. Instead, we must proclaim that Jesus Christ lived the life we couldn't live, died the death we deserved, and rose again to give us eternal life and a new identity. This message must be declared with compassion, urgency, and clarity.

Below you will find common struggles among the least of these, along with relevant Scriptures, Big Ideas for preaching, and brief gospel-centered points to minister hope and healing.

Key Struggles and Preaching Points

1. Rejection and Abandonment

Scripture: Psalm 27:10

Big Idea: Even if others reject you, God welcomes you as His own child.

Summary: Many people in prison and shelters know the pain of rejection from family, friends, and society. Yet the gospel proclaims that in Christ, we are fully accepted and never forsaken. God promises that if *my father and mother have forsaken me, . . . the LORD will take me in* (Psalm 27:10). Jesus Himself experienced ultimate rejection on the cross so that we might be eternally embraced by the Father.

2. Lack of Contact with Children

Scripture: Isaiah 49:15-16

Big Idea: God's compassion for us is even stronger than a mother's love for her child.

Summary: The pain of being separated from children is profound, yet God sees every tear and knows that heartbreak. In Christ, we discover that while human relationships are often broken, God's love is unwavering. He holds us close, engraved on the palms of His hands, and He can bring hope even in the midst of family separation.

3. Worry About the Future

Scripture: Matthew 6:25-34

Big Idea: Jesus teaches us not to worry because our Father cares for us and holds our future.

Summary: The uncertainty of what lies ahead weighs heavily on those in prison or shelters. But Jesus says, *Do not be anxious. . . . Your heavenly Father knows.* When we trust Christ, we discover that He cares for us more than for the birds of the air and the flowers of the field. Our future is in His hands.

4. Resentment and Bitterness

Scripture: Ephesians 4:31-32

Big Idea: The gospel calls us to forgive others because God in Christ has forgiven us.

Summary: Many people have deep wounds from betrayal, abuse, or mistreatment. Resentment can feel justified, but it only poisons the soul. Preach the power of the cross – that Jesus absorbed every offense and offers us the freedom to let go of bitterness and extend forgiveness.

5. Loneliness and Isolation

Scripture: Psalm 68:6

Big Idea: God places the lonely in families, adopting us as His own.

Summary: Isolation is a cruel burden for inmates and those in shelters. Preach that in Christ, we are never alone. God places us in His spiritual family – the church – and promises to walk with us through every valley.

6. Anger

Scripture: James 1:19-20

Big Idea: Human anger does not produce God's righteousness; we need Christ's transforming power.

Summary: Anger often springs from deep hurt and injustice. Point hearers to the one who bore our anger on the cross and gives us His peace. The gospel empowers us to respond with humility and patience rather than with rage.

7. Guilt and Shame

Scripture: 1 John 1:9

Big Idea: In Jesus, we find total forgiveness and a fresh start.

Summary: Guilt haunts many people who have made mistakes that seem beyond repair. But the gospel declares that there is *no condemnation for those who are in Christ Jesus* (Romans 8:1). Preach that no sin is too great for the blood of Jesus.

8. *Addictions and Bondage*

Scripture: John 8:36

Big Idea: Jesus sets captives free; real freedom is found in Him.

Summary: Many people are enslaved to addictions that promise relief but lead to ruin. Preach the liberating power of Jesus, who breaks every chain and invites us into a new life filled with the Holy Spirit.

9. *Feeling Like Second-Rate Persons*

Scripture: 1 Peter 2:9-10

Big Idea: In Christ, we are a chosen people, a royal priesthood; we have infinite worth in God's eyes.

Summary: Inmates and the homeless are often treated as if their lives don't matter. But the gospel proclaims that through Jesus, they are precious, chosen, and have a purpose that transcends any label the world puts on them.

Final Encouragement

When preaching to the least of these, remember:

- Be patient and compassionate. Many people have been hurt by religious hypocrisy and empty words. Show them the love of Christ in your tone, in your presence, and in your message.

- Don't shy away from the gospel. Feel-good messages might comfort temporarily, but only the cross and resurrection of Jesus bring true hope and transformation.

- Invite response and faith. Offer clear invitations to trust in Jesus – not just to hear a sermon, but to encounter the living Savior.

- Pray for the Spirit's power. True heart change is a miracle of grace. Depend on the Holy Spirit to open ears and hearts.

Above all, remember that you are not just preaching to a roomful of broken people; you are proclaiming God's message to beloved sons and daughters, made in the image of God, whom Jesus came to rescue. Your preaching truly matters; and when it centers on the gospel, it will cut to the heart and bring life.

For the Son of Man came to seek and to save the lost (Luke 19:10).

Acknowledgements

We are indebted to several Genesis College team members who dedicated their time and talents to see this book come to life. Dawn Little oversaw the construction of the first draft, helping to build the book chapter by chapter. Dawn is a valuable member of the Genesis team, giving her administrative talents in the production of many courses and book projects.

Fred Bayer lent his careful eyes, making sure we made complex topics easier to understand. His feedback was invaluable. J. D. Valvano provided edits for Part 2 of this book, helping to shape the material. Judy "The Closer" Fry oversaw the final drafts, making corrections and implementing our many "updates." David Johnson dedicated much time to make sure all the parts came together. We are grateful for his consistent guidance, encouragement, and support.

Each person made such significant contributions that this book would literally not exist without their efforts. Thank you! Thank you!

About the Authors

Dr. Johnson   Dr. Woolsey

Dr. Johnson and Dr. Woolsey are founding members of Genesis College and Seminary, an international ministry serving thousands of incarcerated men and women across the nation. They are the authors of *Your Character Matters*, also published by Aneko Press.

Johnson is an ordained minister and has served as the senior pastor of churches in both California and Arizona. He has served as an adjunct professor at several Christian universities. The dissertation for his PhD is a seminal work in the field of volunteer motivation.

Building on his research, several scholars have quoted him and his work in academic journals, including in *Voluntas*, the journal of Johns Hopkins University. Johnson adores his four children – Bethanie, Hannah, Jon Jon, and Daniel – and his six grandchildren.

Dr. Woolsey is also an ordained minister and gifted communicator. He is a lifelong educator who previously served as an adjunct professor at Arizona State University. He has designed courses and has created training materials for several academic institutions, including ASU, Genesis College and Seminary, and Trinity Theological Institute. His training materials are used across the United States and in Mexico and Africa. He is the proud father of Isabella and Dean, whom he loves to the moon and back.

Other Similar Titles

Your Character Matters provides a firm understanding of the spiritual qualifications required to lead God's people. Whether you are the leader of your family, a team at work, or an entire church congregation, this book is for all Christian leaders who want to model Christlike behavior and are willing to make changes in their lives to be great for God.

Available where books are sold.

Investing Wisely is more than a financial guide – it's a call to faithful stewardship. Drawing from timeless biblical principles and the authors' decades of real-world experience, this book equips readers to manage money with purpose and clarity. Whether you're just starting out or looking to reset your financial habits, you'll be guided through seven essential decisions that will help you save, invest, give, and live with eternity in mind.

Available where books are sold.

www.ingramcontent.com/pod-product-compliance
Lightning Source LLC
Chambersburg PA
CBHW021626120626
46545CB00002B/419